BANGOR *in* WORLD WAR II

BANGOR *in* WORLD WAR II

From the Homefront to the Embattled Skies

David H. Bergquist

THE History PRESS

Published by The History Press
Charleston, SC 29403
www.historypress.net

First published 2015

Manufactured in the United States

ISBN 978.1.62619.987.3

Library of Congress Control Number: 2015939775

Dedicated to
James Frederick Dow
Second Lieutenant Air Corps Reserve
U.S. Army
1913–1940

Leader, Aviator, Patriot

James Frederick Dow—official army air corps portrait, 1940.
Bangor Public Library.

CONTENTS

ACKNOWLEDGEMENTS

No project like this is completed in a vacuum; many others contribute with knowledge and resources. I am indebted to Matt Bishop of the Bangor Historical Society; to William Cook of the Bangor Public Library; to the staff of Fogler Library, University of Maine; to Wes Covey and Dave Stonebraker of Hebron Academy; to John Miller, Aviation Artifacts Miller's Field; and to friend Eric Boberg for technical advice. I am also thankful to friends Lee Sirabella, James Stanley and Bette Barker Taverner, now all in their mid- to late nineties, who lived in Bangor through these times and who so generously shared their memories with me. I am especially thankful to friend and fellow historian Richard Shaw for his encouragement and insight. Finally, but not least, I am grateful to my wife, Laureen, who supported me throughout.

INTRODUCTION

A hushed muffle greets each visitor who climbs the twenty-six steps from the street below to enter this lofty chamber. Four large "Golden Lamps," fixtures of burnished brass, cast quiet light on the ceiling above and spill it onto the gray and white squares of marbled floor below. Two mammoth white polished Doric columns streaked with pinks and blues stretch upward to hold the ceiling in place. Near the entrance, a rotunda skylight from far above sheds daylight down on a marble-walled mezzanine and grand staircase trimmed with ornate green balustrades of steel capped by oak. Ample English oak trim and furnishings throughout articulate the building's exalted function. This muted ambiance bespeaks a Grecian temple dedicated to the preservation of the best of Western civilization and culture. The city fathers may have intended to create this milieu when, in 1913, they built this foyer in the new Bangor Public Library after the Great Fire two years earlier destroyed a predecessor building.

A modestly sized high desk with a clear glass cover is placed to the rear of the foyer near the entrance. To its left stands the American flag; to its right stands that of the State of Maine. Within rests the City of Bangor's World War II Memorial Book of Honor commissioned by the city council in October 1944 while the greatest event in the nation's history yet raged. A separate page of the book is devoted to each citizen who fell. A photograph and a narrative of fifty hand-lettered words tell the story of the young person who once walked with us. Each day, library staff turns a page in this sacred

Dedication

City of Bangor
World War II Memorial
Book of Honor

Banqor Remembers Her Sons,
One Hundred and Ten in Number,
Who Died for Victory 1941-1945

Municipal Auditorium, 8:00 PM, 30 May 1947

Planned by direction of the City Council

The front page of the original dedication booklet listing 110 Bangoreans lost in World War II. This number was revised upward to 112. *Author's collection.*

book.[1] The Book of Honor is Bangor's living public tribute to commemorate those lost in a conflict long past.

When a visitor gazes at a page of this consecrated book and looks into the eyes of the person there, he or she will see the light of youth and of personal hope and promise never fulfilled. Snarled by the tentacles of war, a war far from the peaceful banks of the Penobscot, this Bangorean answered the call of a country embroiled in an unsought crisis. "Each day…the faces, the lives, the deeds of these men of Bangor will speak in the silences to us," spoke Reverend Frederick M. Meek at the dedication of the Book of Honor on Memorial Day 1947. "We can never treat lightly…that these men died in assuming the responsibility which we placed on them, and in doing what we asked them to do."[2]

Bangor in World War II: From the Homefront to the Embattled Skies is the remarkable story of a Maine city, of its people and of the soldiers stationed at a large air base within its limits—all of whom answered the call of their country and worked harmoniously together for more than five years for victory. The Book of Honor, in its perfect setting, today symbolizes this great World War II community.

1

A NATURAL AIR CENTER

Two vague spots in the sky suddenly appeared over the southern reaches of the Penobscot River that Saturday afternoon in August 1923. As they drew closer to the old lumber city nestled on the shore's edge, these spots became two large aircraft with wings that seemingly spanned the visible sky. Against puffy white clouds and flying low over sparkling water, these approaching craft fascinated Bangoreans below who were busy shopping. The Martin bombers, with a roar bursting from their two Liberty engines, turned a hard left over downtown buildings and, following the Kenduskeag Stream northward, disappeared over the nearby hills.[3]

Bangor officials expected these aircraft. On August 6, the ever hospitable Albert R. Day, mayor of Bangor, received a note from Captain Lyon of the army's air service about the visit; a recent newspaper article told the public why these warplanes were coming. Still, an aircraft over the city, let alone two flying in formation, was highly unusual and caused a great deal of public stir. Officials expected more aircraft early the next week, as these two were only the advance party of many to follow. And Bangor was about to host an increasingly controversial national figure: Brigadier General "Billy" Mitchell, World War I ace and now assistant chief of the air service of the United States Army. The purpose of his visit was to dramatically demonstrate the ability of the air fleet, based in Langley, Virgina, to defend the East Coast from enemy attack. "The Atlantic coast line is the most vulnerable to attack. The air service can completely cover this great area in seven hours, day or night!" Billy Mitchell exclaimed.

The two Martin bombers, each with a crew of four, put down on the field of Charles W. Morse, a genial Bangorean businessman who was a horse dealer and once had a shop on Franklin Street. He lost his business in the Great Fire of 1911 but reopened on Harlow Street.[1] For twenty-five years, Mr. Morse also owned farmland off Union Street in the Westland Park section sometimes referred to by locals as the Old Mile Race Track. Morse's land was next to the Frank F. Rich farm, and together the contiguous properties provided more than a mile of cleared, flat land. Charles Morse had just finished cutting the hay before the aircraft landed. Once on the ground, the officers properly secured the aircraft while the three enlisted men in the party established an overnight "camp" along Cooper Road. The five officers made their way to the Bangor House for the evening.

That Sunday, many curious Bangoreans headed out Hammond Street to see the aircraft; the buoyant officers and crew welcomed them. But the big show came late Monday afternoon when twenty-one more air service planes flying in three-plane formations appeared in the southern sky. Like the advance party, this larger contingent of approaching warplanes flew low over the Penobscot River and circled over the city while they lined up for landing. Spectators who had gathered earlier at Morse field watched in awe as the aircraft, one by one, landed with ease. Meanwhile, other citizens rushed out to Hammond and Union Streets to see this historic event. By the time the twenty-one additional planes were on the ground, thousands of Bangoreans had gathered there. Besides thirteen Martin bombers, the contingent also included eight De Havilland scout planes, each with a two-man crew. For the most part, these aircraft, including the two bombers that had arrived Saturday, represented the entire air defense arm of the United States. Mayor Day drove out to the field that afternoon and warmly welcomed all the airmen to Bangor.

The ever dramatic Billy Mitchell was nowhere to be seen; he was still in York Harbor, Maine, with his fiancée. Major John N. Reynolds visibly commanded the squadron of warplanes, but Billy Mitchell really directed the entire landing from an unknown wireless station. He arrived in Bangor on Tuesday morning and at first inspected the base camp. Then Mitchell left for downtown, along with his officers and the mayor, who had driven out once again to the field, so that he could speak to the Rotary Club at its weekly meeting at the Tarratine Club. There, Billy shared his views about the importance of aircraft in future wars. His ideas were highly controversial in the early 1920s and flew in the face of conventional military thinking during a period when Congress routinely cut military budgets amid growing isolationism. Mitchell contended that future wars would be fought and won in the air and that the country with the greatest air force would win. Consequently, he advocated a strong air arm for the United States and one that would be independent of the army. And he put Bangor on the defense map of the country because of its northeastern location when he said that the city was a "natural air center"; he predicted a great air future for the Queen City.

The War Department already had Bangor in its sights as a strategically located area prior to Mitchell's speech that Tuesday afternoon. For the War Department, Bangor's location in eastern Maine elevated the area's national defense value, particularly if attacked by European powers. In late August 1922, the War Department sent Lieutenant Charles H. Howard of the air service to scout out landing areas in Bangor. Coincidentally, however, Billy Mitchell happened to be on a motor trip through the state and met with Howard in Bangor. Mitchell was unlikely officially assigned to assist Howard, but he certainly expressed his views with him before continuing on his way to Moosehead Lake for some fishing. He and Howard determined that the Morse field site was what was needed for national defense in this corner of the nation.

A strong weather front with numerous showers and strong winds came through the area late Tuesday. Mitchell's crews tied down the Martin bombers and De Havilland scout planes. The following day was clear and fall-like with blustery winds. Many Bangoreans took advantage of the improved weather to view the aircraft. Billy Mitchell returned to Morse Field in Mayor Day's car Wednesday morning. Major Reynolds, though, decided that it was still too windy to leave the field as scheduled, so the air fleet remained tied down. The weather conditions, however, did not deter Billy from lifting off without some risk in his colorful De Havilland pursuit plane, which he dubbed *Osprey*—its green pennant flying from the tail.[5] Bangoreans, who admired Billy's natural mahogany plane with its unique decorative touches unlike the other pursuit planes, watched in awe as he disappeared into puffy clouds.

The night before, hospitable Bangoreans had hosted a special dance for the visiting celebrity aviators at the Chateau Ballroom on Kendusdeag Mall. The delay in the scheduled departure gave the servicemen a chance to visit the Bangor State Fair at the fairgrounds off Main Street, where the airmen hoped to see a featured air act by two stunt pilots, Merle L. Fogg and George M. Sparks. Both men had visited them at Morse Field earlier; Merle Fogg held the first pilot's license issued by the State of Maine. The strong winds that day, though, prevented the aerial daredevils from performing.

The air fleet took off from Morse Field Thursday with the exception of two bombers that left the following day. For Bangoreans, that week was dominated by air excitement. Aircraft were a new technology for Americans, and their appearance generated a great deal of local public interest across the country. Bangor was no exception. Four years earlier, citizens had seen an army aircraft when Major A.H. Gilkeson, along with his mechanic, Master Sergeant H.M. McGraw, landed a Curtiss biplane on Morse's hayfield in August. Major Gilkeson described his flight up from Rockland in his flimsy flyer as the most harrowing experience of his flying career because of the seemingly endless Camden mountains that loomed in front of him as he flew northward. In the late summer of 1924, the people of Bangor saw another military aircraft for several days as it flew over the area taking photographs of possible landing fields. Lieutenant James H. Doolittle piloted this specially equipped De Havilland. Jimmy Doolittle went on to have a storied career in the army air corps and later the army air forces, the nomenclative successors to the air service. The diminutive but daring Doolittle was a pioneer in instrumentation flying. Years later, he achieved fame for leading a group of sixteen B-25 Mitchell bombers off the pitching and bobbing deck of the aircraft carrier USS *Hornet* in an April 18, 1942 retaliatory air strike of Japanese soil, the first ever.[6] Still, it was many years before military aircraft in any number landed on Bangor soil.

Despite all the ballyhoo surrounding Billy Mitchell's visit, Bangor showed little aviation progress by the mid-1920s. Bangoreans, not unlike most Americans, still viewed airplanes and air travel as a novelty. The lure of the Jazz Age, the prosperity of the Roaring Twenties and the good times to be had despite Prohibition preoccupied most people. Tired of the lofty preachments of Wilsonian democracy and scarred by the horrors of trench warfare that their doughboys experienced in the Great War, Americans turned their backs on world involvement and embraced isolationism. Bangoreans, likewise, looked inward and preferred a daily life they could control. Fortunately, a few prescient thinkers saw beyond the immediate and recognized the economic potential of the aircraft. One such Bangor citizen was Edward R. Godfrey, a prominent lawyer and descendant of an old and respected local family.[7] From early in his youth, Godfrey was fascinated with the experiments of the Wright brothers and their early flying attempts. Godfrey understood the physics behind flying; he also understood how aircraft could benefit his city.[8]

Late in October 1925, Godfrey bought the nearly ninety-acre Morse farm with the intent of developing an airport as a private venture. He then

Among the 1926 members of the Bangor Chapter of the National Aeronautic Association are Lieutenant Rowell (third from the left) and Lieutenant Lowell (seventh from the left). *Richard R. Shaw.*

leased his land to two ex–World War I flyers, Lieutenant H.W. Lowell and Lieutenant Fred W. Rowell, who formed a company, Maine Air Service, Inc., to advance aviation in Bangor. Lowell served as president of this new venture and also established a flying school with offices on Central Street. At Godfrey's field, Lowell planned on giving flying lessons, conducting aerial photography and surveys, "carrying" passengers and providing all kinds of commercial flying services.[9] Rowell, Lowell and Godfrey became active members in the National Aeronautic Association of the United States, an early advocacy group for the advancement of aircraft and air travel. Godfrey served as president of the Bangor chapter.

Major General Mason M. Patrick, chief of the army air service, lent credence to Maine Air Service's ambitious plan for airport development. Like Mitchell, he saw Bangor as important to national defense and as a natural location for an air service reserve. However, in those days of military retrenchment, General Patrick said no money from Washington was forthcoming to help develop

The Bangor Airport circa 1934. *101st Air Refueling Wing, Maine Air National Guard.*

an airport. Still, plans went ahead, and Governor Ralph Owen Brewster broke ground for a runway in early April 1926. Godfrey, though, funded the airport's early development. Over the next twenty years, Ralph Owen Brewster remained a consistent booster for a viable Bangor airport as he moved up the ranks of Maine politics to U.S. senator.

By 1928, the Maine Air Service disappeared from the Bangor scene, and the fall of 1929 ushered in the Great Depression that poignantly altered the lives of most Americans in some way. At the fledgling airfield, several years of lease and business arrangements followed, along with some unrealized business ventures. Still, physical progress by the early 1930s was steady, and the airport featured a gravel runway, a modest hangar and a few small mechanical shops. Godfrey remained a steady advocate for air travel to Bangor throughout this period and added to the acreage of the airport when he purchased the contiguous Rich farm.

Entrepreneurial pilots on a Sunday in mid-October 1930 advertised rides for Bangoreans for as little as one dollar. This enticement along with the day's beautiful fall weather brought one thousand citizens to Godfrey Field, some for their first ride ever in an aircraft. Nearby Fairmount Park residents complained to the police about the planes as they skimmed over their rooftops; the police ordered the pilots to fly "higher up." This public show of interest in aircraft and flying, however, rekindled new attempts to put Bangor on the air transportation map. The next spring, the chamber of commerce took the lead in an effort to introduce commercial passenger service to the city when it stated that the city was "behind the times" and brought in A.H. Waite, an airport specialist from the department of commerce, to view several sites within the city limits for a municipal airport. These included Godfrey Field and the City Farm. Wait recommended Godfrey Field because of the amount of suitable flat land, its proximity to a highway and its lack of obstacles or hazards to flying. By this time, the locally owned Crymble Aircraft Corporation, to whom Godfrey had leased his field, had made many improvements to facilities that allowed larger, more technologically advanced aircraft to land; planes were now larger, flew faster and provided greater passenger comfort. Bangor was ready for modern times.

Boston-Maine Airways, Inc., a joint air passenger service of the Boston and Maine and Maine Central Railroads, announced that it would begin daily flights into Bangor on August 1, 1931. This enterprise arranged with Pan American Airways Corporation to provide the aircraft. The daily schedule included two flights to Boston—each way two and a half hours long. The airline used a Fokker Tri-Motor twelve-passenger plane to make the trip. A symbolic inaugural flight on July 31 introduced Bangor to its first air passenger service. Hundreds of Bangor dignitaries, including Godfrey, attended the inaugural flight. This new route also introduced the first airmail service to Bangor.

Pilot James Crane gave "her the gun" on that August 1 morning, and the Fokker lifted off for Boston with four passengers, two of whom were local newspaper reporters along for the ride. One of these men described the flight as having "the feeling of merely floating through space in a leisurely manner." The airline shut down these flights, though, in September, stating that they were only a summertime operation, but the real reason was poor public acceptance and the worsening Depression. Boston-Maine Airways attempted a second try at introducing regular passenger air service in 1933. Now, with the help of National Airways, the railroads conjured up a major publicity event to encourage flights into Bangor on their airline service. Amelia Earhart, famous aviatrix of the 1920s and '30s, flew into Godfrey Field at the controls of one of two Stinson tri-motor ten-passenger aircraft on Wednesday morning, August 9, 1933, to introduce the airline's renewed

Boston-Maine Airways Fokker Tri-Motor, 1931. *John Miller—Vintage Wings.*

service. When Amelia landed shortly after noon, hundreds of curious Bangoreans and assembled city dignitaries greeted her. Earhart and officials soon left under police escort down Hammond Street and then on to Union Street to the Bangor House for a special luncheon. There, Amelia, in brief remarks, thanked Godfrey for his efforts over the years to provide a "suitable landing field in Bangor" and then mildly scolded women as the greatest force of "resistance that aviation had to overcome." She encouraged women in Maine to take advantage of the opportunity now to fly out of Bangor. After a hurried lunch, she posed with city leaders for photographs and then left for the airport for a 2:30 p.m. departure.

Encouraged by Bangor's recent positive air publicity, the city council entered into lease negotiations with Godfrey for his airfield with the intent to further develop the site into a municipal airport with the help of some federal funding then available. Godfrey was initially agreeable but, due to some local politics, withdrew his lease offer. Godfrey and the City of Bangor finally came to terms a year later with a lease agreement that allowed the city to move forward with aggressive plans for modernization to keep up with advances in the aircraft industry. Meanwhile, Amelia Earhart returned to Godfrey Field on Sunday, August 12, 1934.

Amelia Earhart with dignitaries at the Union Street portico of the Bangor House, August 9, 1933. Edward R. Godfrey is at the far left in the first row. *Richard R. Shaw.*

Amelia's second trip to Bangor was called Woman's Day, an event arranged by the chamber of commerce in cooperation with Boston-Maine Airways. Planes of the air service flew nearly empty out of Bangor, a fact lamented by Godfrey himself. A commonly held perception was that the wives of businessmen perceived flying as dangerous and thus discouraged their husbands from using aircraft for business trips. This belief hindered the growth of air passenger service. Amelia hoped to dispel that notion. Organizers issued a preset number of free tickets for a demonstration ride to local women, many of whom were married to prominent businessmen. Each of the twenty-seven demonstration flights of short duration over the city aimed to convince women that flying was safe. The flights began at 9:45 a.m. and concluded by 4:15 p.m. The weather was perfect for flying with little wind and clear visibility. Once airborne, Amelia visited with each passenger, chatting with the ladies about the advantages of flying while her pilot, Milton H. Anderson, maneuvered the craft over the city. Mrs. Parthenia Cameron, at eighty-one years old, was the oldest participant and quipped

Amelia Earhart with participants in Woman's Day, August 12, 1934. *John Miller—Vintage Wings.*

that she thought flying was "just grand." Joanne Jordan, the ten-year-old daughter of *Bangor Daily News* publisher Fred D. Jordan, was the youngest. Amusingly, flight number six was not all made up of female guests. Ralph Mills, a local theatrical impersonator, somehow acquired a ticket, disguised himself as a woman with the name of Miss Sally Miller and boarded the aircraft. Once aloft and as Amelia approached to chat, Ralph pulled off his wig and stated, "I wanted to ride with you, so I just came along." The aviatrix took the joke in good humor and later posed with Mills for pictures. The long day was a genuine success and helped to advance the safety of flying in the minds of many Bangorean women.

With a lease arrangement in place, the city moved forward with modest improvements to the airfield funded by federal dollars; the city spent little of its own money. Boston-Maine Airways introduced continuous airmail service with a contract from the U.S. Post Office in 1934. In September 1936, the airline replaced its Stinsons with new Lockheed Electras, the latest in aircraft design. The Lockheed was heavier, more powerful and equipped to fly at night. The use of these advanced aircraft demanded improvements to the airport. The city worked with Godfrey to add more land not already under lease primarily for runway expansion and other improvements; then it sought funding from the Works Progress Administration (WPA), a work relief agency instituted by the Roosevelt administration to provide work for unemployed Americans. The city appropriated $30,000 for airport improvements in January 1936. The federal government appropriated $68,000. Godfrey signed over legal possession of the two existing runways that May. By June, the WPA started work in earnest to improve the airport by expanding the length and width of the runways, installing lighting to include a rotating beacon and illuminated wind indicator for night flying, building a radio beam station and adding amenities to the airport's administration building, which was the hangar Godfrey built in 1931.[10]

By the late 1930s, the alluvial plain through which Birch Stream lazily meandered like a slowly slithering snake until it plunged into the Kenduskeag had become the site of a modern airport serving a vibrant

Work begins on 1936–37 airport improvements. Hammond Street is in the foreground with Cooper Road running almost parallel with the main runway. *Bangor International Airport.*

Maine city. Early aviators and advocates saw the potential of this land on the western side of the city. World events and the need for improved national defense soon transformed the Bangor Airport into a facility the average Bangorean hardly imagined.

2

AN ADEQUATE DEFENSE

Increasingly, front-page newspaper stories covered the panoply of elevated world events. President Franklin Delano Roosevelt in a January 4, 1939 speech to Congress sounded an alarm and called for an "adequate defense" for the nation. He defined this defense as having three parts: increasing the armed forces, locating key facilities and strengthening citizenship. For this last point, Roosevelt specifically meant that the American people needed "the imagination and devotion that give the staying power to see things through."[11] Much would need to be done; the American army ranked thirty-ninth in the world.[12] Still, Americans wanted to stay out of evolving conflicts in distant lands.

The breakout of war in Europe on September 1 somewhat jolted Americans' current worldview into a new reality. Congress, still clinging to its isolationist policy, however, only modestly modified its neutrality position. Undaunted, FDR asked Congress in January 1940 for nearly $2 billion, an astronomical sum then, to shore up America's defense.[13]

A crucial part of this defense was the construction of air bases to protect strategic areas of the country from attack. Governor Sumner Sewall, a World War I aviator, already knew the importance of aircraft to defensive warfare; he advocated for the construction of an air base in Maine because of its "strategic importance as the country's 'Atlantic outpost.'"[14] Ralph O. Brewster, representative to Congress from Maine's third district and a former governor, introduced a bill in Congress in late April that directed the secretary of war to establish such an air base in Maine. FDR called on Congress the next month to provide funding for fifty thousand planes annually as key to defense.

Bangoreans read and heard all this news, as did the rest of America. The slowdown in the European war early in 1940, sometimes referred to as the Sitzkrieg, cast doubt on what America should do. Later that spring, though, the Nazi juggernaut resumed, and European democracies began to fall like dominoes before the German war machine. Congressman Brewster in a May speech to the Bangor Lions Club supported the building of an army air base in Maine, stating, "Maine, as the nearest point to Europe, with a series of land areas that are convenient stepping stones, must realize that we cannot expect indefinitely to remain aloof." Barely a week later, Brewster, a strong champion of airport expansion in Maine since his days as governor, hosted a group of individuals from the Civil Aeronautics Authority (CAA) as they surveyed potential air base sites in Maine. The strategic location of Bangor's airport in eastern Maine with its nearby abundant available land for potential expansion put the city's airport at the top of the survey list. Shortly thereafter, the CAA recommended the Bangor airport as the site for a new Maine air base.

Despite what seemed like a green light to proceed with the project, a last-minute snafu developed between the Bangor City Council; the State Defense Commission, which supported the Bangor site; and the administrator of the Works Progress Administration, John C. Fitzgerald. Fitzgerald claimed that the city council and defense commission did not approve of the runway plan drawn up by the WPA—the federal governmental agency that would build the base—and the plan for the acquisition of additional land; he threatened instead to look at Oxford Plains or Presque Isle as the preferred location. However, the War Department was anxious to get a strategic base underway because of the worsening international climate and had little patience for local politics. Congressman Brewster personally became involved in Washington and lobbied for an amicable resolve. On Monday, August 19, the *Bangor Daily News* carried the headline "Army Giving Bangor Green Light as Air Base." The city council and WPA in subsequent meetings later that week ironed out remaining issues. The crisis was over.

The collapse of France in June left England as the only European democracy to oppose Hitler. Many Americans thought England was doomed and that America would be next. It was a pivotal point in national history.[15] The question about what America should do in response to the growing international crisis was hotly debated in the presidential campaign that summer, including in Bangor. Early in September, Colonel

Theodore Roosevelt Jr. spoke to a packed city hall crowd at a GOP rally and accused his distant cousin FDR of leading the country into war. He was particularly upset with FDR's swap of fifty American destroyers with the British for naval bases—a deal FDR worked out without Congress's involvement. Former president Herbert C. Hoover, unfairly accused of causing the Great Depression, stated emphatically to delegates at the GOP convention that the United States must stay out of the current war unless the western hemisphere was attacked. Hoover, though, also said that "the hope of mankind and the hope of civilization is that democracy survive on this continent." On this point, he and FDR agreed. Always the master politician, President Roosevelt seemed to express the majority of Americans' prewar sentiments when he said at a September campaign stop in Tennessee, "If we are to survive, we cannot be soft in a world in which there are dangers that threaten Americans—dangers far more deadly than those the frontiersman had to face." This particular event was his dedication of the Great Smoky Mountains National Park. The president further expounded on his analogy of current history by comparing it to the time of the frontiersman when he said, "The earth has been so shrunk by the airplane…that Europe is closer to America today than was one side of these mountains to the other when the pioneers toiled through the primeval forest."

Back in Bangor, the pace of air base construction picked up. Lieutenant Colonel Arthur R. Wilson, a representative from the War Department in Washington, and other dignitaries from the army general staff visited the airport in Bangor in late August. The group assured the city council of the federal government's commitment to build the base, and quickly. In turn, the city moved expeditiously, as part of its agreement and financial commitment, to acquire the additional land needed for expansion. A crew of seventy-five workers started work on extending the two existing runways on September 5. More workers soon followed and started building an entirely new third runway. The three runways gave Bangor a Class IV airport, the highest governmentally rated airport for those days, and were built to support the weight of the army's new bombers. The city finished its acquisition of 640 acres by mid-October, the biggest parcel being 450 acres belonging to Godfrey and including land he had previously leased to the city. City manager James G. Wallace, in a speech to the Lions Club in September, called the airport development on Hammond Street one of the largest military and commercial air bases in the East and the fulfillment of "the dream of years" for the city.

The already rapid pace of development further accelerated when the War Department announced in early October that the 43rd Bombardment Group (Heavy) and the 8th Air Base Group would be stationed in Bangor with an assigned strength of over 2,500 men. The War Department released more specifics on its $1,683,387 air corps facility in December. It listed the building of barracks, mess facilities, officer housing, an administration building and an infirmary. One day later, four army engineers from Boston showed up on the site and began surveying. Wearing gloves, winter coats and hats, the engineers braved the cold and worked rapidly from dawn to dusk for five straight days, including Sunday, before returning to Boston. They carried back with them city maps showing sewer lines, water mains and other infrastructure.

Bangoreans followed the airport development in the local media. Domestic events that year, though, emphasized the country's other moves toward an adequate defense. On September 1, President Roosevelt activated units of the National Guard for a one-year period of active duty. The War Department ordered the 240th Coast Artillery from Maine to train at Portland. More call-ups would follow. More telling of future events was Congress's enactment of the first peacetime draft law in the nation's history. FDR signed this historic legislation on September 16 that called for the registration of approximately 16,500,000 men between twenty-one and thirty-five years old for potential mandatory military duty. The president called this law necessary for the United States to avert "the terrible fate of nations whose weakness invited attack." The law required state governors to establish local draft boards to oversee registration. The local draft boards would select men from their jurisdiction to fill the quota for their area. FDR selected Wednesday, October 16, as the day for national registration.

Bangor held its draft registration in the municipal auditorium on Main Street. Schoolteachers manned the twenty-five banquet tables set up along one side and at the end of the hall. Schools were closed and flags put out; the auditorium opened at 7:00 a.m. and closed at 9:00 p.m. At the end of the day, city clerk Archie R. Lovett reported that 3,157 eligible Bangor men had registered. This number was more than 10 percent of the city's population. Each man who registered was issued a draft board card on which was printed a serial number. Should that number be drawn, the registrant was "drafted." Two weeks later, Secretary Henry L. Stimson drew the first number for the new draft from the same bowl used for World War I. Maine's quota for this first round of the draft was 80. Of that number, 10 completed induction at the Bangor Induction Headquarters on Central Street on November 18. They left immediately for a year of military service at Fort Devens.

On the editorial page of the *Bangor Daily News* for New Year's Day 1941, a cartoon depicted a stern Uncle Sam seated in a chair before a young bare boy representing the New Year and asked, "What are you going to do about the condition of the world?" The New Year boy replied, "I'm asking you!" In Bangor, nobody was asking that question! People were taking action. In fact, that same newspaper displayed a picture of Governor Sumner Sewall of Maine inspecting a large bulldozer at work at the airport. And on January 6, 1941, the federal government opened bids for the massive air base construction project; it would be the largest in the city since the rebuilding of downtown after the Great Fire of 1911. Now called a cantonment, the specs called for the initial construction of 97 buildings out of a total of 150 planned. The War Department appointed Lynn V. Spink of the U.S. Army Corps of Engineers in charge. Spink moved to Bangor, taking up residence on French Street. With his assistant, Earl F. Stanton, and a small team of laborers, Spink scurried over the area laying out streets and building sites. The building contract required completion of all structures in ninety-five days. Early estimates for the needed manpower to do the job called for over four thousand laborers; Spink worked with the state employment office on Harlow Street to secure the workers.

Five companies submitted bids. On January 28, the War Department awarded T.W. Cunningham Inc. of Bangor the contract. This contract covered the A, B and C sections of the cantonment. Earlier, the War Department awarded a contract for a one-million-plus-gallon standpipe (water tower) to the Pittsburgh–Des Moines Steel Company. Washington had yet to decide on contracts for Section D, which called for a large hangar and twenty other buildings that included machine shops, storage buildings, a control tower and a parachute building. Once the project began, the War Department made additional contract decisions on needed infrastructure.

Cunningham began work on the project on Monday morning, February 10, after he received the final approval from the War Department. Ralph O. Brewster, now a U.S. senator from Maine, continued to expedite the project. Sections A and B included barracks, each housing 63 men, for up to 2,350 soldiers. Also included in these two sections were mess halls, recreation buildings, administration buildings, storehouses, an exchange building, a central fire station and a theater. Section C called for officer quarters, an officer mess building and a complete hospital compound that included several ward buildings, as well as a number of other support structures.

Left: *From left to right*: Lynn V. Spink, U.S. Army Corps of Engineers; First Lieutenant Leo Moore, adjutant, U.S. Army; and Harry F. Dunbar, chief engineer, Army Field Area Number One. *Bangor Historical Society.*

Below: Mud at the main entrance to the Bangor air base, now Northeast Drive. *Bangor Public Library.*

Meanwhile, the War Department awarded the D.A. Sullivan Company of Northampton, Massachusetts, the contract for the buildings in Section D for a total of $288,551. Work on that section of the air base began on February 19. Work on the runways, under the direct supervision of the WPA, continued. The Carlo Bianchi Company of Natick, Massachusetts, began to construct the water and sewer systems.

The cantonment buildings took shape off Hammond Street as quickly as mushrooms pop out of the ground in Maine's damp, dark forests. Crews of carpenters and laborers completed the first building in just two days. Spink used it as his office and directed the massive building project from there. Workers next set cement piers below the frost line for the barracks and other support buildings in the A, B and C cantonment sections. The pace of construction continued on target despite the severe cold of midwinter that threatened to explode the cement and the occasional snowstorm that usually deposited up to a foot of snow that workers had to clear.

The greatest weather challenge Spink and his workers faced began in mid-March, when the ground began to thaw. This natural process produced a "sea of mud" as workmen and machines traversed repeatedly over thawing ground. In some cases, workers employed ingenuity to deliver supplies to building areas within the cantonment. Where trucks bogged down, workers used horse-drawn sleds to accomplish the needed tasks and to keep the project on target. Any visitor to the cantonment area risked becoming immersed up to his or her ankles in mud.

Workmen at the cantonment site. *John Miller—Vintage Wings.*

Workmen using a horse-drawn sled to deliver building supplies. *John Miller—Vintage Wings.*

Lynn Spink dealt not only with mud, he also dealt with potential labor problems. Electricians on the job and workers for the Bianchi contract threatened labor stoppages. However, all parties, in the spirit of getting the work done within Washington's allotted time frame, met and resolved their issues. By mid-April, the mud had dried, and nearly two thousand workers, half of the original estimate needed, pressed ahead to complete the buildings in Sections A, B and C.

Throughout the spring, Spink hosted nonstop inspections. The sound of hammers had just started when Senator Brewster toured the cantonment site. General John B. Brooks, commander of Westover Field in Massachusetts, visited and lunched with Spink. (The Bangor Air Base, in the air corps' original plan, served as a forward airdrome for defense under the control of Westover Field.)[16] Then in late April, dignitaries representing the WPA and Maine Defense Commission reviewed the progress of construction. Daily, sixty-six on-site inspectors, made up of army engineers and civil service workers of the U.S. Engineering Department, inspected the lumber, plumbing, electrical installation and concrete placements. They reported

Bangor Daily News reporter Spencer Winsor going after a story. *Bangor Public Library.*

their findings to Spink. But the inspection Spink wanted occurred on Monday, May 12, when inspectors from the War Department visited for two days. The visiting officials accepted the project as completed on that Wednesday, ninety-two days after its beginning and three days ahead of schedule. Now, with the barracks and operational buildings completed, the cantonment was ready for soldiers except for running water. Workers rushed to complete the one-hundred-foot-tall, forty-two-foot-diameter standpipe on the modest hill behind the cantonment. Once completed, workers pumped water up to it from a brick pump house; water was supplied from a city line and from a well sunk on site.

Meanwhile, less than a mile back toward downtown off Hammond Street, workers constructed housing for married officers and noncommissioned officers on Thirteenth Street in an area called Hayford's Field. Many cantonment workers migrated there to build the eighteen two-apartment and nineteen six-apartment buildings after they completed their work on the air base; the H.P. Cummings Construction Company of Ware, Massachusetts, had the contract with the Federal Housing Administration for the half-million-dollar project. On the western outskirts of the city,

A completed barracks for sixty-three soldiers. *Bangor Public Library.*

The air base standpipe today. The rotating white and green beacon that sat on top is now in the Maine Air Museum. *Author's collection.*

Fairmount Terrace on Thirteenth Street, now Hayford Park. *Bangor Public Library.*

the twenty-eight-acre Hayford's Field was once the home of the semipro Highland A.C. baseball team; the open land remained intact as Bangoreans built modest homes around it. The contractor left the old baseball diamond as a playground for the children of air corps personnel. Officials named the new subdivision Fairmount Terrace; Bangoreans called it G.I. Village.

West of the cantonment, construction work continued on the buildings in Section D and on the runways. Residents watched, fascinated by the rapid transformation of the western side of their city.

3

JAMES FREDERICK DOW

Bangoreans watched with pride mixed with apprehension as members of their own 152nd Field Artillery of the Maine National Guard marched by on their way to Union Station. The citizen soldiers appeared resolute and determined as they kept in cadence to the beat of their band. Uncle Sam called them up for a year of active duty; they soon left by train for Camp Blanding in Florida. Two days before, on George Washington's birthday, their city hosted a "farewell party" at the auditorium.[17] Ironically, no one mentioned Washington's farewell admonition to his countrymen to stay clear of "foreign entanglements." On February 24, 1941, observers saw the 152nd's departure then as only part of the country's defense preparedness effort. The crowd's mood that day was similar to that of a few months earlier when, on Armistice Day, military units marched by grimly serious and business-like. The troops reflected that "the world was no longer…safe for democracy, and that many of the principles which the day commemorates…are in the gravest danger in world history."[18] The holiday-like atmosphere of the previous generation who marched off from Bangor to the Great War twenty-three years earlier had disappeared. All across America, this solemn scene was repeated.[19] And some parade watchers might have remembered that previous June, when the local papers carried the story of one young soldier they knew: James Frederick Dow.

Even as a lad, James Dow displayed gifted athleticism with daring. No organized sport seemed beyond his mastery, a trait that distinguished him from his peers beginning with his years at Houlton High School. Shortly

The 152nd Field Artillery marching to Union Station for departure, March 15, 1941. *Richard R. Shaw.*

after his birth on November 20, 1913, in Oakfield, where his father was a brakeman in the railroad yards, his family moved to Houlton, twenty miles to the northeast and the seat of Aroostook County. His father, Henry, was moving up the ladder in the Northern Division of the Bangor and Aroostook Railroad; he later became superintendent. There, the young family settled into a large "Bangor Box," a version of the American foursquare design, on Green Street. The family grew. Three years younger than James was his sister Norma, with whom he was very close; followed by his brother, Harold, by another three years; and finally, his sister Gloria. Thirteen years separated her from James. His mother, Sarah, or "Sadie," was doting; his father, Henry, was distant. Yet the home seemed full of fun and activity.[20]

James was also a jokester. When Gloria was born and as the doctor was leaving the house, his ten-year-old sister Norma said to James, "Now I know what they carry in that bag." Of course, James had egged his younger naïve sister along in explaining where babies came from. He teased Norma about that statement for years.[21] Many years later, while home from college, James asked his mother and Gloria to pick up some cigarettes for him while they were downtown shopping. A quick trip turned into many hours, and when the pair finally returned to the house on Green Street, James met them at the front door disguised as an aged and grayed old man to emphasize what their loitering had done to him.[22] In high school, he learned the art of impersonation; he often imitated Charles Boyer, a 1930s popular film star, to the delight of his friends. He acted in school plays and was president of the school's drama club.[23]

The five-foot, eight-inch, well-built youth[24] with thick dark hair gained the attention of the fairer sex; James's ability to dress in the latest fashions also drew the attention of his classmates. They predicted, in a yearbook spoof, that in his future, he would manage a beauty parlor in town. But James had other ideas. As did so many young men of that time, he spent idle time making model airplanes. He hung the completed models from the basement ceiling of the family home and dreamed of flying. How he was going to make that happen remained unknown.

It was in his high school athletic feats where James gained the attention of a wider audience. He played about every sport Houlton High School offered, including basketball and baseball. He was extremely fast, a skill he applied in a 1930 track meet with Presque Isle; he came in first in the 100, the 220-yard dash and the hurdles.

He applied this speed to football as well. In one early 1930 fall game, again with Presque Isle, James caught the ball and outran the backfield fifty yards for a touchdown. He performed the same way in a later game with Caribou that season. Undeterred by a previous play in which he had recovered the ball and raced forty yards to the goal line but which was discounted due to a technicality, he grabbed the ball in a play and raced to the thirty-yard marker, throwing it to a team member on the goal line for a touchdown. James's daring and quick thinking earned him the admiration of onlookers. He soon became known in the local press as Houlton's "Speed King."

It was the height of the Great Depression in 1931 when James graduated from Houlton High School. No jobs were to be had. He wanted to go to college but needed to improve his preparation for university work. He enrolled in Hebron Academy that fall and stayed for two years in postgraduate study. There, he also played football, where he "put up a good game," and ran track as "one of our great track stars." He acted in the drama club's productions and was president of the outing club.[25] He then applied to the University of Maine and was accepted for September 1933.

James was more mature and more serious when he entered the university that fall. The world, too, was rapidly becoming more serious. Hitler had come to power, and the Japanese were eying further Pacific expansion. But Orono seemed a long way from Europe or the Far East. Immediately, James became involved in the many athletic opportunities. There, he participated in indoor track his first fall semester and amassed many points at various meets. He also joined the freshman basketball and football squads. His athletic abilities quickly came to the attention of Black Bears football coach Fred Brice. By his sophomore year, James was on the varsity team playing the halfback position. He was a team player, yet he became known as a great kicker and an outstanding passer. In his spare time, James spent long hours practicing these skills on the athletic field next to Memorial Gymnasium. His efforts paid off in the fall of his senior year in a football game for the state series title with Bowdoin College. James, in a daring move, grabbed the ball from the hands of a Maine player about to be buried by onrushing Bowdoin linemen. He then ran into Bowdoin territory unchallenged. On the next play, Maine scored when James pulled off a "Statue of Liberty" play in front of hundreds of onlookers, including many Bangoreans gone mad with excitement.

James Dow's high school graduation portrait, 1931. *Author's collection.*

James's quiet and unassuming mannerisms, coupled with his athletic notoriety, gained him many college friends. He became a brother at Phi Gamma Delta fraternity in his sophomore year. Still, James liked to play a joke or two. One night while roaming the campus with his friend Joe Hamlin, James talked Joe into letting him press his pants with an idle steamroller parked in front of Colvin Hall.[26] College antics aside, he showed his serious nature as a student in ROTC, the Reserve Officer Training Corps program. The university, as a land grant college, required that every male student have two years of compulsory military training; the junior and senior years were optional. James stayed on with ROTC and joined the elite Scabbard and Blade Society made up of only upperclassmen. Upon graduation, members were eligible to join the army reserves. James served as president during his

Drawing by James Dow of Bangor and Aroostook Railroad Steam Engine #253, winter 1937–38. *Author's collection.*

senior year, an experience that allowed him to employ his leadership abilities and teamwork skills learned in organized athletics. He enjoyed the structure and regimen that military life offered. It was predictable and sure, so unlike the world James faced when he graduated in June 1937.

James joined the army reserves after college and spent some time that summer at Fort Williams and Fort McKinley near Portland. He returned to Houlton that fall. He had no job as the economy continued to languish. His father, unable to offer anyone else a job, declined to bring him into the Bangor and Aroostook Railroad organization because he thought it would be unfair. So that long, cold, snowy winter, James spent hours in the basement of the family home making train cars out of tin cans and expanding a train set that his brother Harold had given him. It was a fine replica, detailed and exact. His railroad drawings also demonstrated his penchant for precision.[27]

The world situation continued to deteriorate. Japan swept down the Chinese coast, and Hitler continued to re-arm Germany. The U.S. military increasingly became alarmed and realized its inability to defend the nation. General Henry "Hap" Arnold, chief of the air corps, knew that the country needed to increase its pilot pool for defense. Knowing that the army then lacked training facilities to teach young men to fly, he contracted with civilian flying schools to take on military recruits and teach them to fly. One such school was the Parks Air College in East St. Louis, Illinois. In early 1939, this school recruited James, as a member of the reserves, to enter a flying class there.[28]

At Parks, James enrolled in a nine-month curriculum that included mornings flying in a Stearman biplane with afternoon classroom instruction in navigation, aeronautics and meteorology. School officials named James a cadet captain because of the leadership abilities he demonstrated. James then moved on to the air corps' college-like facility at Randolph Field in Texas. Here, in a training period called "Basic," James flew the BT-13, a low-winged monoplane. He learned instrument and night flying techniques. Again, school officials recognized his leadership skills when they named him a cadet sergeant. The final phase of flight training, or "Advanced," was at nearby Kelley Field. There, he flew the faster, more advanced AT-6 aircraft and satisfactorily completed all the increasingly sophisticated instruction. On March 23, 1940, he earned his wings and was commissioned a second lieutenant in the air corps reserve of the U.S. Army.

His folks were unable to see him pinned with his wings as Texas was too far from northern Maine. In a March 19, 1940 letter to his folks, James reflected on his accomplishment: "I'm at a point in my young life that I surely never had in mind a year or two ago. I know I talked a little Air Corps several times, but not until I got into it did I think seriously of it. I don't want anything anymore right now." He then thanked his parents: "I can't help but think…of you folks at home and what it took to put me here. I've had 400% more help now than I was entitled to…I hope that someday I'll be given the chance to show you what it has meant to me and how I feel about it now."[29]

After a few weeks of additional training in Georgia, the air corps assigned James to Mitchel Field on Long Island, New York. There, he joined a bombardment squadron flying Douglas B-18 bombers, a derivative of Douglas's DC-2 and main army bomber in 1940. Monday, June 17, seemed perfect for flying and formation practice despite a slight smog and haze over New York City to the west. The squadron of four bombers left Mitchel at about 8:00 a.m., flying northwest over Queens until they gained an altitude of two thousand feet and an air speed of 150 miles per hour. The squadron came together in a diamond formation and readied to perform a defensive maneuver. It was extremely important for bomber crews to learn formation flying, as the tightly knit groups best fended off enemy fighter attack by concentrating maximum protective gunfire. James was flying copilot with Lieutenant Paul Burlingame, a West Point graduate and football star, in the pilot's seat. Their bomber occupied the left corner of the diamond formation. Lieutenant Richard Bylander was flying his B-18 in the forward point of the diamond, while Lieutenant Leroy Stefonvicz was flying his bomber in the right point of the diamond. Lieutenant James Ellis followed behind in the rear point position of the diamond formation. Lieutenant Ellis soon radioed Lieutenant Burlingame, the flight's leader, that he wanted his copilot to take over flying his bomber. Lieutenant Burlingame decided that this was a good time to do a "cross-over turn," a maneuver in which the bombers would trade position within the diamond formation. The flight leader ordered Lieutenant Stefonvicz to move from the right position and to take the lead. This move required Lieutenant Bylander, whose bomber was already in the front of the formation, to slip back to the left, where Burlingame's aircraft was positioned. Simultaneously, Burlingame, to make way for Bylander, needed to move over to the right corner of the diamond formation, thus performing a cross-over turn. What should have been a routine maneuver went terribly wrong. While moving rearward and to the left, Bylander's plane dipped down and locked wings with the Burlingame bomber. In this process, the whirling propellers ruptured wing fuel tanks, and the flaming bombers crashed to the ground. Both bombers hit the ground only several hundred yards apart in a new Queens suburb called Bellerose. Spectators below, including many housewives doing their Monday morning laundry, watched in horror. Bylander's plane crashed in a grassy median strip, narrowly missing nearby houses. Burlingame's bomber crashed in the driveway of a house on the next street over. Mayor Fiorello La Guardia, himself a World War I flyer, heard the commotion on his car radio as he made the trip back to New York City and immediately went to the Bellerose neighborhood. After viewing the carnage, he remarked, "See here. That fellow [Bylander] tried to land. See where he skidded along the road. He did not want to hit those houses." He said the same of Burlingame's plane the next block over. In their last moments, pilots and copilots of both planes worked valiantly not to crash into houses. Only one resident became a casualty the next day, when she died from the effects of severe burns. Eleven airmen, five in the Bylander aircraft and six in the Burlingame aircraft, were dead. James Dow was among them.[30]

News of James's death reached the Dow home shortly after noon. A friend of James had seen the story come over the news wires where he worked, and he called the house at 34 Green Street. When Sarah, his mother, heard the news, she said, "No, it couldn't have happened, the sun wouldn't be out."[31]

That Friday, Houlton witnessed the funeral of a favorite son. At noon, a caisson carried James's casket from the Episcopal church through the city to Evergreen Cemetery. The Maine American Legion was meeting in Houlton at the time and stood in salute on the sidewalks as the funeral procession passed. Those who watched could see firsthand the price a dangerous world exacted.

4

THE SURVIVAL WAR

Events that spring were hurried and befuddling. A few months before, Bangoreans watched the Battle of Britain unfold in their newspapers. Now in early 1941, the fighting in Europe shifted to North Africa and the Balkans. FDR delivered his "Four Freedoms" speech to Congress in January and set out lofty goals for the United States.[32] What would happen next? At home, work had just started on the army's cantonment on Hammond Street when the first soldier, Henry L. Hartwell, was recruited and assigned to an ordnance company at the air base in Bangor. It was a premature assignment, as no military personnel were there; he was sent on to Fort Devens. A few weeks later, seven army recruits appeared. They enlisted in Philadelphia, traveled to Camp Lee in Virginia, picked up their uniforms, reported to Bangor and walked into Spink's field office on Fuller Road. They traveled 1,300 miles and found no army here. Dubbed by the local press as "Army Orphans," personnel of the 152nd Field Artillery headquarters put them up in the armory on Main Street until the army untangled this latest snafu.[33]

Even at the higher echelon level, confusion abounded. General John B. Brooks, commander of Westover Army Air Base in Massachusetts, visited in late March and announced that the first commanding officer of the Bangor base was Lieutenant Colonel Ulysses G. Jones. Lieutenant Colonel Jones and family arrived in early April and moved into a residence on Boutelle Road. Just a few days later, the army officially announced that Lieutenant Colonel Jones was not the new base commander, but rather Colonel Carl W. Connell was to take command. Lieutenant Colonel Jones, instead, was the executive officer at the air base. Colonel Connell left Puerto Rico, where he commanded Borinquen Field, and arrived in Bangor by train on April 8. A few days earlier, a Major Raymond M. Barton of the quartermaster corps, the second officer on duty at the base, showed up and began his work. Second Lieutenant Paul L. Riley arrived three days later and was the purchasing and contracting officer.[34] First Lieutenant Foster B. Perry, the base's first chaplain, then appeared, but as if to keep the shuffling going, the army reassigned him a few days later to Mitchel Field.

The A, B and C sections of the cantonment were incomplete when the first troops of the quartermaster corps arrived at the base on April 25 in a twenty-two-truck convoy from Westover Field. The night before, these fifty troops of the 241st Separate Quartermaster Company (Air Base) bivouacked at Fort Williams in South Portland. The quartermaster corps' function was to set up and supply the new air base. QM soldiers had their first lunch in Bangor in a field off Fuller Road. Then, soldiers moved into one of the just-completed barracks, but they had to carry water three hundred yards from a temporary spigot and use field latrines because water service into the cantonment was not yet connected. Corporal Frank Butterfield of Bangor was among this group of soldiers. Now, the total number of soldiers at the base stood at sixty-four men. This was a modest beginning for the almost six thousand men and women who eventually populated Bangor's air base.[35]

Through the month of May, additional soldiers began to trickle in and report to the base. The quartermaster corps worked feverishly setting up bunk beds, lockers, kitchens, offices and other needed facilities. The army ordered reserve officers to report for active duty, some with dependents in tow. They had to find temporary housing, as the military housing at Hayford's Field was still unavailable. Meanwhile, the army engineers hosted an open house of the A, B and C sections of the cantonment for the public on the afternoon of Sunday, May 18. Nearly five thousand Bangoreans toured the new "city" that had popped up in their midst. Spink and other army corps of engineers members served as guides as the crowds marveled at what they saw. Visitors met few soldiers; most were busy setting up facilities that were not on the tour.

The largest contingent of troops to date arrived at Bangor's Union Station on June 4 in a special troop train from Langley Field, Virginia. The six-car Pullman train took two days to reach Bangor and held 226 men of the 8th Air Base Group and others in the medical department. These troops boarded fifteen army trucks from the base. Bangor police, sirens blaring, escorted the

Soldiers of the 241st Separate Quartermasters Corps (Air Base) having their first lunch in Bangor. *Bangor Public Library.*

convoy as the trucks chugged their way up the Hammond Street hill to the base a mere mile and a half away. More troops from Langley Field arrived by automobile that Saturday. Throughout that summer, more soldiers found their way to Bangor. Spink, meanwhile, had the Cunningham Company sheath all the newly constructed buildings. This additional insulating board changed the army's designation of the buildings from purely "temporary" to "more or less permanent."

West of the cantonment, the Sullivan Company neared completion of Section D. While this section comprised twenty various buildings, the most impressive was the all-steel hangar capable of housing the largest bombers then available to the air corps. Workers finished that section by July 22 without problem. Completion of the runways, though, posed difficulties. The final runway plan, initially a source of controversy with the city fathers in 1940, called for the extension of both existing runways, which had been upgraded in 1937. Then, the north–south runway was extended to 2,200 feet while the east–west runway was extended to just over 1,800 feet.[36] In order to meet the Class IV airport standards, both these existing runways needed to be

The 226 soldiers at Union Station on June 4, 1941, say, "Hello, Bangor." *Bangor Public Library.*

widened considerably and lengthened to 5,000 feet. A new runway needed to be constructed from the corner of Hammond Street and Cooper Road all the way to Fuller Road, nearly a mile in length. Beginning in the fall of 1940, truckers hauled in 130,000 cubic yards of gravel, or the equivalent of thirty-five mile-long freight trains, from the Bradford Pit and the Stearns Mill area of Hampden.[37] From the air, the new runway pattern looked like a large letter A with runways now labeled as going from northwest to southeast (the old north–south runway), east to west (the old east–west runway) and northeast to southwest (the new runway). This pattern took advantage of prevailing winds. The WPA was in charge of construction. The runways crossed each other at various points. As the construction neared completion in the spring of 1941, army pilots flying in the first planes to the base reported a "hump" at these intervals because of a slight change in grade at the intersections of the runways. This situation was unsatisfactory for the large bombers soon to be stationed at the base. WPA's Fitzgerald brought the work to a jarring halt in mid-June. Workers immediately began work to remedy the problem by either raising or lowering the grade of the runways at these crucial points. Truckers brought in additional gravel while 250 workers and equipment operators worked around the clock. Among these workers were 29 Native Americans from the Penobscot Nation in Old Town, who traveled by bus to the worksite each day.

Other infrastructure projects moved ahead at a spiraling pace to prepare the base for army occupancy. The Bianchi Company completed a two-mile outfall sewer line southeast across the city farm to the edge of the Penobscot River, where untreated sewage from the base was dumped. The New England Telephone and Telegraph Company fully equipped a new telephone building with seven dedicated lines, the latest in switchboard design and auxiliary power units in case of emergency. A U.S. Post Office was opened on the base, and the J.R. Cianchette Company constructed a 400- by 1,600-foot concrete apron for aircraft parking near the large hangar. Colonel Connell, keen to eradicate hazards that may endanger flying, oversaw the removal of a barn and two vacated houses and the clearing of trees and bushes, all of which were within 2,500 feet from the ends of the new runways. Even abutting property owners patriotically removed trees that could pose a hazard. Workers also placed overhead electrical and telephone wires underground in these areas. The Maine Central Railroad built a spur line into the base area from its main line at Northern Maine Junction more than a mile away in Hermon. This spur extended a half mile into the base on the western edge of the cantonment. Prior to this, contractors trucked in all construction supplies and materials from nearby railroad freight yards in Bangor. The Pelkey Motor Transport Company, which brought in over ten thousand tons of supplies and building materials to the site during the construction phase, trucked in sixteen twenty-five-thousand-gallon gas tanks for installation by the Cianchette Company. These tanks held the necessary one-hundred-octane aviation fuel for the aircraft Washington soon assigned to the base. To provide incoming and outgoing aircraft with radio communications, the army purchased a 400- by 600-foot tract of land for a radio station from the Bangor and Aroostook Railroad two miles away off Route 2 in Hermon. Spink directed the construction of a large coal storage area to service the base's heating equipment. The army blocked off the Cooper Road entrance from Hammond Street. Eventually, this road disappeared from all Bangor maps. And while the War Department continued to alter and expand the base into the future, for the time being, the base seemed complete.

The worsening international situation contributed to the rush of construction of the air base. In the third week of June, Hitler turned on his would-be friend Josef Stalin of the Soviet Union and launched a massive invasion into the Ukraine region toward the Russian steppes. Not to be

The author explores the beginning of the railroad spur into the base. This mile-and-a-half-long track carried hundreds of tons of supplies into the base during the war. *Richard R. Shaw.*

outdone, Japan moved into French Indochina a month later. Bangoreans, as did most Americans, wondered what would happen next. A strong defense seemed appropriate while helping friendly nations with Lend-Lease that Congress adopted earlier that spring. Now, Bangor's $3 million plus air base stood ready as part of the nation's defense network. Colonel Connell pushed to have Bangor's new air base designated a "critical defense area" by the

Aerial view of World War II Dow Field, circa 1944. Hammond Street is in the upper left, and Union Street is in the lower right. *Bangor International Airport.*

government, which would mean that the needs of the base would receive greater priority. The government approved his initiative in keeping with FDR's late May declaration of an unlimited state of national emergency. This designation for Bangor also meant that the new air bases being constructed in Aroostook County, one in Presque Isle and one in Houlton, would be auxiliaries to Bangor.

Lynn Spink left for Aroostook County in late July to assist in the building of air bases there. Spink was a "can-do" person. No physical obstacle seemed insurmountable to this army engineer. That April, Colonel Connell, another "can-do" person, joined Spink; together the two men oversaw the dynamic change to the former Westland Park area of the city from windswept open land to a major air facility in the nation's defense system. Spink, with his vast engineering background, and Connell, with his considerable army administrative ability, were able to make the project happen and just in time.

Preparations by the quartermaster corps for the arrival of more soldiers sped up that summer; the inspections also picked up pace. This time, the highest-ranking military and government officials visited the new army air base in Bangor. Over Memorial Day, Lieutenant General Delos C. Emmons, head of the army's air corps, visited and expressed pleasure at the progress he saw. Major General Henry H. Arnold of the air corps and army deputy chief of staff followed two weeks later. (Personally taught to fly by the Wright brothers in 1907, General Arnold over his career witnessed the growth of American air power and played a crucial role in the coming war.) A flight surgeon accompanied General Arnold because of his troublesome heart—a practice that became standard when he traveled by air. General Arnold ate that evening at the Tarratine Club and stayed overnight in the Bangor House. Just two days later, Major General Herbert A. Dargue, chief of inspectors for the air corps, followed. He returned later that summer. In mid-June, D.F. McCauley, director of airways and airports of the WPA in Washington, D.C., toured the facilities accompanied by national, state and local officials. WPA's chief engineer, Perry A. Fellows, inspected the airport in mid-July, and General Dargue returned in early August for a two-day inspection. General Dargue, a friend of Colonel Connell, now commanded the 1st United States Army Air Force. This change in title reflected Congress's reorganization that summer of the air corps into several army air forces. Dargue personally flew the Douglas C-47 transport plane, a military version of the DC-3, into Bangor. At the end of his tour, the general stated that he was "personally delighted" at what he saw and reiterated the strategic importance of Bangor to the nation's defense.[38] Finally, Major General Francis Wilby, commanding officer of the First Corps Area of the U.S. Army headquartered in Boston, arrived on August 23 for a quick visit.

Bangor's air base was now ready. Personnel of the 43rd Bombardment Group arrived in late August to its new station in Bangor. Special troop trains from Langley Field brought in more than one thousand soldiers over the next few weeks. Troop convoys being escorted up Hammond Street became a common sight to Bangoreans. And the new military housing complex at Hayford's Field on Thirteenth Street officially opened, ready for its first families. With the 43rd came the 8th Air Base Group, which was an installation support and administrative unit; a weather section; an ordnance company; a mechanical detachment; as well as other smaller but needed military support units. Additional medical personnel also arrived. The sprawling base hospital, with four wards capable of holding twenty-five patients each, was located on the hill known to locals as Hersey Woods and lay behind the rest of the cantonment. Hospital staff, including a flight surgeon and a dentist, ministered to the medical needs of assigned soldiers, gave inoculations and conducted physical examinations to prospective air corps cadets.

Four-ward hospital at Dow Field. *Bangor Historical Society.*

The first aircraft also arrived. Earlier that spring, Lieutenant Colonel Jones, primarily for publicity purposes, arranged for an A-17, a 1930s fighter plane and no match to the sleek German and Japanese aircraft, to be flown in from Mitchel Field. The 43rd, however, brought in a complement of already-obsolete B-18 Douglas Bolo bombers and the B-17A, which was the earliest version of this later famous aircraft. The bomb group also flew in several two-engine A-29 Lockheed Hudsons.

Bangor welcomed its new residents. As the air base filled up with 2,500 soldiers, citizens saw more and more soldiers about town. The small city on the Penobscot suddenly swelled in size by nearly 10 percent. In mid-May, the Tarratine Club, a men's social club founded by well-to-do Bangoreans after the Civil War, hosted a "good-will" reception and dinner for those air corps officers already assigned to the air base. Bank presidents, newspaper editors and influential businessmen, among others, were keen to know about their new neighbors. Colonel Connell, always gregarious, drew the interest of many as they engaged him in conversation bursting with questions. This initial encounter set a positive tone that marked many years of friendly

A Douglas B-18 Bolo bomber. *United States Air Force.*

relations between the military installation and its civilian neighbors. Bangoreans fully welcomed and embraced military personnel.[39] Soon, residents, in small but meaningful ways, helped their new neighbors. The Bangor YMCA made it known that the base needed recreational equipment. Alice Brown responded by donating a pool table. Others gave books, games and magazines. Before he left for an assignment at Mitchel Field, Chaplain Perry indicated a need for home visits, especially over the upcoming Fourth of July holiday. The local response was overwhelming as Bangoreans invited homesick troops to spend the holiday with them. Local organizations planned socials and dances for soldiers. The Ava Maria Circle hosted a dance for soldiers in mid-July. In August, the American Legion Boys' Band gave a concert for the soldiers on the base, and many Bangoreans donated furniture for base day rooms and recreation halls when that need was made known. The army's friendly outreach to the community for its support of troops continued that fall when Chaplain Shea, Roman Catholic chaplain, spoke at a Unitarian conference in mid-October and encouraged continued civilian help for the welfare of soldiers. The YWCA hosted "teas" for army wives living at the new Hayford's Field military housing complex now called Fairmount

Terrace. Colonel Francis B. Valentine, commander of the 43rd, also spoke to the Bangor Business and Professional Women's Club explaining his unit's mission.

State senator John E. Townsend of Bangor organized the city's largest "welcoming" event for October 24 in conjunction with the newly formed local Soldiers Welfare Council, an organization composed of several civic and charitable groups. Members sought ways to help soldiers at the air base feel welcome and happy. They planned a number of recreational events throughout the coming winter, the welcoming party being the first. Edgar N. Keith, leading Bangor businessman and state bowling champion, served as ticket chairman. Mrs. Edward R. Godfrey served on the planning committee. More than 2,500 soldiers and citizens attended the gala affair held at the Main Street municipal auditorium. Governor Sewall and his wife and Colonel Connell and his wife were honored guests. In brief speeches, Louis Fleming, chairman of the Bangor City Council, pledged "every effort" to make a soldier's stay in Bangor happy. Colonel Connell praised the "teamwork and cooperation" of the military and the city to "keep 'em flying," the new air corps slogan adopted earlier that spring. Governor Sewall, a World War I flyer, encouraged the continued hospitality of Bangoreans, as army "men need the extra lift." He also advised listeners that, in the coming months, not only soldiers needed to sacrifice for national defense but also citizens.

Air base soldiers frequented local eateries, stores, theaters and other businesses that fall. The YMCA welcomed the use of its facility by soldiers at no cost, and many soldiers visited the Bangor Public Library. A few even tried out for parts in a play being produced by an evening high school class. An active local United Service Organization, formed under the auspices of the Soldiers Welfare Council, increasingly offered off-base activities and programs for soldiers. Many women from Bangor and Brewer, Bangor's neighboring city on the east side of the Penobscot River, raised money over the summer of 1941 to open a USO facility and to offer programs. Volunteers placed mite boxes in banks and stores. Adeline and Caroline Wing hosted a garden party at their estate on State Street. Eventually, citizens raised enough money to purchase a large home at 11 West Broadway to house USO activities. Sprague Adams built the eighteen-room, three-floor house in 1860 on a oversized lot. Within one mile of the air base, this facility provided the space USO organizers needed. The USO began operations with an open house on Sunday, November 23. The first floor included a lounge and music room, a library reading room, an office for the director and assistant and a snack bar located in the kitchen. The second floor housed game rooms for pool and ping-pong and a room exclusively for writing. The third floor offered a darkroom, an art and crafts area and classrooms. Throughout the facility, the local USO committee created an atmosphere of a "home away from home"—a welcome center for soldiers. The local USO subscribed to the purpose of the national USO: "It is an American conception, just as it's thoroughly American that the leisure-time needs of the military forces should be met by the people themselves, instead of through government regimentation."[10]

At the air base that fall, military activities increased. Ordnance units from Westover Field arrived in early September for several days of maneuvers. The army sent men from the base to participate in maneuvers elsewhere. Flying activity also increased, marred by an occasional mishap, such as when the landing gear of a B-18 gave way upon landing due to pilot error. The most serious mishap, however, was the crash of a bomber bound for Bangor from Langley Field on November 15, 1941. Fog enshrouded the air base and caused the pilot, twenty-eight-year-old Lieutenant Peter W. Beckham, to overshoot it. He continued to fly northeast for sixty miles until short of fuel. When he realized his mistake, he tried to bring his aircraft down in what may have looked to him like a field. The deceptive fog hid the true identity because it was in reality a burned-over hilltop in a desolate section of Springfield. Beckham tried to correct his lapse in judgment at the last moment, but his right wing hit the ground and spun the plane into a catapulting somersault. The impact broke off the cockpit from the rest of the aircraft and hurled the four young airmen out, killing them instantly. Rescuers had to hack their way nearly four miles through the wilderness to bring out the airmen's bodies to the Passadumkeag River, where rescuers transported them by canoe ten miles down to Morrison's Mill in Burlington. Base Chaplain Shea, who just a few weeks earlier celebrated the opening of the base's new chapel, accompanied the sixty-man army detachment. This crash reminded Bangoreans reading gruesome local newspaper accounts that the defense of the nation was dangerous business.

The world situation only continued to worsen. In early November, Congress, in response to increased Nazi U-boat attacks on American shipping in the North Atlantic, amended the 1939 Neutrality Act and permitted the arming of U.S. merchant ships. Secretary of State Hull's talks with Japanese ambassador Kichisaburo Nomura that demanded Japan's withdrawal from China stalled.[11] At least the completed Bangor air base was an important link in the country's new defensive posture. Bangoreans, like millions of other Americans, wondered what was next. They soon found out. Indeed, over the next several years, they learned what President Roosevelt meant when he later described these times: "There is one word that we could use for this war, the word 'survival.' The Survival War. That is what it comes pretty close to being—the survival of our civilization, the survival of democracy, the survival of a hemisphere."[42]

5

BANGOREANS HUNKER DOWN FOR WAR

The weather that Sunday morning in Bangor started out fair and mild, but temperatures began to cool down by midday. As many returned from morning services, a brisk wind picked up, as if to remind Bangoreans of the winter that lay ahead. Still, religious citizens looked forward to the festive holidays of Hanukkah or Christmas. More than 5,500 miles to the west, just as the sun began to rise there, Bangor's own Carlton Orr worked at preparing breakfast for his fellow soldiers stationed at Hickham Field just across from Ford Island, Pearl Harbor. Hickham Field was one of one hundred plus army air forces installations like the Bangor air base that now existed for defense across the United States and its territories. Like so many young men of that time, Carlton enlisted in the army only a few months after graduation from high school. Carlton was a member of the class of 1939 and particularly excelled in debate and represented the school in debating tournaments. He did well for himself in the army and now was a head cook. Back in Bangor, Frances and James Stanley had the radio on that afternoon at their Division Street apartment when, at 2:30 p.m., the program was interrupted by the announcement that Pearl Harbor was under attack by the Empire of Japan. For the Stanleys, this news seemed unreal, as they had anticipated that a war-precipitating event would come from Germany. Frances, in the mid-1930s, studied in Germany as a dance student with world-renowned dancer Mary Wigman. Frances personally witnessed the rise of Hitler and the goose-stepping march of German youth in the streets.[43] By this time, Carlton lay dead as the result of an exploding Japanese bomb that in the first wave of attack hit the mess hall where he served breakfast. The damage was so catastrophic that rescuers never located his body.[44]

The War Department placed the Bangor air base on alert that afternoon. Colonel Connell sent out military police to order all personnel not on base to return at once and requested all theater managers to announce the same to soldiers in their audiences. No soldiers were on the streets of Bangor that Sunday evening.[45] Army officials at Fort Devens dispatched an additional cavalry unit to Bangor to provide increased security at the air base. Base officials restricted civilian vehicles from entering the base and closed the field to the general public. The army restricted all nonmilitary use of the air base except for Northeast Airlines, which served the airport. From now on, other aircraft had to use the Old Town airport, to include the university's Civilian Pilot Training Program (CPT). Local radio station WABI set up a temporary broadcasting station at the *Bangor Daily News* offices on Exchange Street to bring news to listeners about the latest events occurring half a world away. And the next afternoon, President Roosevelt delivered his rousing "day that will live in infamy" speech to Congress in which he requested a declaration of war on Japan. Congress quickly complied. On December 11, Nazi Germany

Main Street in downtown Bangor looking north toward West Market Square, 1943. *Author's collection.*

and Fascist Italy declared war on the United States. Congress reciprocated. In a matter of a few days, the country was at war on two fronts.

The city of Bangor, like its resident military base, moved quickly and affirmatively to strengthen its defenses. Curtis M. Hutchins, director of the already established Civilian Defense Committee, worked with the city manager and aided the city in quickly implementing defensive measures. Now afraid of sabotage, city manager Fred D. Farnsworth ordered that guards be placed at the waterworks and advised owners of industrial plants to place guards at their factories. Farnsworth also called for Bangor citizens to register for newly created volunteer civil defense positions. By that Tuesday, more than 250 Bangoreans—men, women and high schoolers—had registered at civil defense headquarters in city hall. The city implemented a partial blackout the next evening by turning off some streetlights and shutting off the lights illuminating the Thomas Hill standpipe. Later, as weather allowed, the city painted its brilliant white iconic standpipe an olive drab.

Over the first few days after Pearl Harbor, local newspapers carried stories about many Bangoreans thought to be in harm's way. Anxious family and friends sought news about their loved ones, but in these confusing times, they could do little. What they could do was volunteer for defense, and volunteer they did. More than one hundred young men flooded the army recruiting station on Central Street in the first two days after Japan's attack. Potential air raid wardens jammed the city hall's auditorium later in December to learn about the plan to protect the city and how they played a crucial role. Earlier, Farnsworth had outlined his air warden plan at a Kiwanis Club meeting and stressed that while Bangor lacked any large industrial plants, it did have an air base within its boundaries—a perfect target for enemy bombers. By December 13, the city had released its air raid warden plan to the public. The city appointed Gordon D. Briggs as chief air raid warden. The plan divided the city into three districts, each with a district air warden in charge supervised by Briggs. In turn, within each district, the plan called for enough warden posts to cover five hundred inhabitants. Each warden post was manned by an appointed senior warden with three to five assistants. Finally, the plan established a "Report Center" supervised by the chief air raid warden and to which all district wardens channeled communications. The city modified this plan somewhat when it scrapped the three districts in favor of using the boundaries of the seven existing political wards. Now, each of these wards represented an air raid district. The plan further subdivided ward three into two districts, thereby making a total of eight air raid districts. A minimum of three hundred air raid wardens were needed.

Bangor City Hall at the corner of Hammond and Columbia Streets. *Richard R. Shaw.*

Bangor City Council in its first meeting of the new year characterized itself as a "war council." In accepting the chairmanship, Frank O. Youngs said that "these were grim times" and pledged that Bangor would do all that was necessary for the war effort. Indeed, the war news for early 1942 was grim. Japanese forces overran Manila, forcing American troops onto the Bataan Peninsula. German U-boats were sinking American vessels on the country's eastern seaboard. The nation struggled to transform itself into a fighting force.[46] In Bangor, Chief Warden Briggs announced the selection of the district air wardens. A twenty-five-hour course to train volunteer air raid wardens was underway and included ten hours in first aid taught by the Red Cross, five hours in protection techniques from poison gases, five hours' instruction about incendiary bombs and five hours in general responsibilities. Bangor schoolteachers taught the last fifteen hours of this course provided they had attended a two-day school held early in January at state civil defense headquarters in Augusta. Briggs established a Report Center in the basement of city hall.

By early March, the city had more than one hundred qualified air wardens. More were on the way. Their role increased in importance as the war progressed. At first, they had to canvass their ward to make sure that constituents complied with "blackout rules" issued by the governor. They also visited each dwelling to register people in each, distribute the blackout rules, inspect each dwelling for blackout shades and suggest safe places in case of a bombing attack. Officials encouraged residents to get to know their air raid warden as a neighbor, and the *Bangor Daily News* ran a brief biography of each warden. By that summer, more than five hundred air raid wardens were at work and proudly wore air raid warden patches.

Bangor put into place other defense measures that spring. The city arranged for the Red Cross to offer citizens, particularly women, courses in nursing aid, home nursing, motor corps (auto mechanics) and canteen operation. The police and fire departments trained additional auxiliary policemen and firemen for emergencies. The city ordered air raid sirens to be strategically placed around the city, the largest of which was placed on the roof of the newly opened Court Street police headquarters. Defense officials determined and labeled the location of downtown air raid shelters, the largest being in Freese's Department Store, Sears and Roebuck and city hall. The school department had workers cover a number of interior school windows to deter flying glass and placed sandbag barriers around the lowest exterior windows of all schools. Workers completed this work at the Fairmount School first because it was the nearest public school to the air base and the most vulnerable in case of enemy attack. Workers also sandbagged certain lower windows of the public library. The fire chief surveyed the twenty underground water reservoirs in case of emergency should the water system be damaged in a bombing raid. Bangor had built these cistern-like structures in the mid-nineteenth century to fight fires, prior to installing a water hydrant system. Each contained anywhere from twenty-five thousand to forty thousand gallons.

Civilian defense officials conducted the first tests of the air raid system early in the spring. These initial tests used a call system to determine the time volunteers took to reach their duty stations. Officials then conducted the first blackout tests. Initially, these tests were announced in advance in the newspapers; tests often divided the city into a section east of the Kenduskeag and a section west of the Kenduskeag. At first, the city used the street fire alarm systems already in place along with the city hall bell to sound the blackout alarm since the air raid sirens had not yet been installed. Air raid wardens then checked their area to be sure citizens complied by turning out lights or by lowering special blackout shades. The city turned off streetlights while auxiliary police stopped traffic and directed motorists to turn off their lights. Police also required pedestrians to extinguish their cigarettes and to seek shelter. Bangoreans took these tests seriously, and both Hutchins and Briggs generally expressed satisfaction with the results. Later tests were unannounced and more sophisticated.

The level of activity at the air base picked up considerably after Pearl Harbor. Lieutenant Colonel Francis B. Valentine, commander of the 43rd Bombardment Group, ordered increased training flights for his pilots. Now that the country was at war, Colonel Valentine knew that it would be only a matter of time before the 43rd would be deployed overseas. One of these training flights went amiss on December 18, 1941, when a B-17A Flying Fortress crashed on takeoff. Witnesses reported that as the aircraft reached takeoff speed on the lengthened five-thousand-foot east–west runway, one of the wings hit the ground, pivoting the speeding plane into a ground loop. The careening bomber skidded down the runway on its fuselage until it came to a flaming stop. Runway guards ran to the stricken craft while crash wagons raced to the scene. Nine crew members struggled to escape through doors and hatches before the fully fueled bomber exploded. The pilot became wedged in the escape hatch in the cockpit roof, but Privates Harold V. Keahey and Wilson S. Smart, disregarding their own safety, jumped onto the burning craft and pulled the pilot to safety. This heroic action, seen on Bangor's own soil, was repeated countless times in the war years to come. (Later in the summer of 1942, the War Department awarded the Soldier's Medal to Privates Keahey and Smart for their heroism.) While this scene played out on the east–west runway, three A-29 Lockheed Hudsons of the 43rd returning from submarine patrol circled above and delayed their landing on another runway until the Northeast Airlines flight from Boston landed.

Soon after the turn of the year, the War Department ordered the 43rd Bombardment Group deployed to the South Pacific to take up station to harass the Japanese and impede their continued expansion. The bombardment group left Bangor in February 1942 for the Southwest Pacific via Cape Town, South Africa. There, the group became part of the 5th Air Force.[47] Other changes occurred at the air base. Colonel Carl Connell, the base's first commander, left for a new assignment in Washington, but not before he changed the name of the Bangor air base on January 23, 1942, to Dow Field in honor of James F. Dow. Connell took this action consistent with official protocol and policy. Army air forces headquarters in Washington forwarded three names to him, and he made his choice. Earlier that summer, city manager Farnsworth had indicated to Lieutenant Colonel Jones, the first executive officer at the base, that it was the desire of the city council for the new air base to be known as the Bangor Air Base. Colonel Jones, however, soon left to take over command of Westover Field; Farnsworth's request went unanswered.[48] It was twenty-six years before the city council's wishes were satisfied. Yet in the spirit of wartime patriotic fervor and in remembering who James Dow was, Bangoreans cheered the new name for their air base.

While the U.S. Army was busy at Dow Field, it was also busy in Bangor when it established a filter center. Bangor's civil defense chief Hutchins, on behalf of the army, called for one thousand volunteers to man this center twenty-four hours per day, seven days per week. The purpose of the filter center was to monitor airplane activity over nine-tenths of the state of Maine and parts of the maritime provinces of Canada. In the days before coastal radar, this human watch system was extremely important for coastal defense. A large cadre of "plane spotters," trained by the army in aircraft identification, scanned the skies for any aircraft and called in sightings to the filter center, where officials identified the aircraft in question. Should an aircraft not be immediately identified, the filter center relayed a warning to one of six district warning centers in the state of Maine, which in turn relayed that warning to cities and towns within their jurisdiction. Bangor's district warning center was located in the boardroom of the Bangor Public Library. Meanwhile, the army dispatched interceptor fighter aircraft from Dow Field to determine an aircraft's identify. Within the filter center itself, a volunteer wearing a telephone headset took the call of an air spotter and plotted the location of that aircraft on a large map. Volunteers continued to plot the track of that aircraft as they received more reports from plane spotters. This intricate air warning system in Bangor was part of a network of filter centers along the East Coast of the United States and was under the command of the army's Boston air defense wing. Later in the war, a contingent of WAACs (Women's Army Auxiliary Corps) supplemented volunteer manpower.

James Stanley recalled his time as a plane spotter in Bangor. He watched in two-hour shifts each Friday night from an observation post on the sixth floor of the Exchange Building on State Street. This post, equipped with special

The domed Bangor Public Library with Bangor High School to the left. *Author's collection.*

distance viewing devices and high-powered binoculars, looked south over the confluence of the Kenduskeag and Penobscot Rivers toward Brewer. There, Stanley and other volunteers watched for unidentified aircraft.[49]

Enemy planes appeared over Bangor in late April 1942 and dropped incendiary and gas bombs on downtown. Air raid sirens and alarms wailed as civil defense volunteers sprang into action. Auxiliary and regular firemen raced to Main Street to extinguish burning magnesium. Mustard gas bombs near Union Station prompted a unit of soldiers from Dow Field to put on protective clothing and gas masks. A bomb through the roof of Eastern Maine General Hospital did not faze doctors and nurses there; they knew what to do to protect patients. Red Cross workers and volunteers established casualty stations at John Bapst High School and at the Fifth Street Junior High School to treat those wounded, represented by Boy Scouts. Other theoretical incidents marked this practice drill of Bangor's civil defense plan. Local defense officials and state observers deemed this first practice mobilization a success. Bangor was now ready to defend itself.

Bangoreans intensely followed the war news in local newspapers or on radio broadcasts by WLBZ or WABI. That spring, the *Bangor Daily News* distributed special supplements produced by the Associated Press titled *World Wide War Book* and, later, *Behind the War News.* People read with glee about General Doolittle's daring raid on homeland Japan by B-25 Mitchell bombers launched from the deck of the heaving aircraft carrier USS *Hornet.* Still, the war news was bleak. World War I ace Eddie Rickenbacker, personal friend of Maine governor Sumner Sewall, warned that the United States was losing the war. Indeed, in an impromptu speech delivered standing on the wing root of his Douglas passenger plane at the Bangor airport on June 1, 1940, Rickenbacker had warned America to stay out of the war unless invaded.[50] Now, he urged the nation to give up "selfishness, greedy ideas and petty politics and go to work—not for eight hours a day or forty hours a week, but fifty, sixty and seventy hours a week." According to Rickenbacker, the country needed to go to work for victory. In Bangor, that was already happening.

Bangoreans worked for victory through personal initiative and through their established civic organizations. Only a few days after Pearl Harbor, the Bangor Police Association voted to purchase $10,000 worth of defense bonds. Citizens generously contributed in early 1942 to the American Red Cross War Fund, exceeding its quota for the city. And later that year, the chamber of commerce, in cooperation with the American Legion, organized auctions through its membership. Chamber members donated items, to which they assigned war bond values. The bidder might bid $25

Edgar N. Keith reading in the living room of his home at 10 Boynton Street and listening to the radio. *Author's collection.*

Downtown storefront advertising an upcoming auction. *Bangor Public Library.*

for an item, essentially pledging to purchase a war bond for that amount. Organizers then gave the successful bidder the item in question. Over the course of the war, other civic groups followed suit, donating the proceeds to various war relief funds.

By far the biggest community efforts toward victory during the war were the war bonds and war stamps campaigns. This effort got a big boost with the visit of Dorothy Lamour to Bangor on September 17. Affectionately referred to as "America's Bond Bombshell," Lamour traveled to Bangor through the auspices of the War Activities Committee of the Motion Picture Industry. In 1941, more than one million soldiers at 202 army posts voted her their favorite subject for "foot locker art."[51] Ms. Lamour arrived by train at Union Station that afternoon and was immediately escorted by a military honor guard to a 4:45 p.m. outdoor rally at Bass Park. Bangoreans purchased tickets to this event by buying one dollar's worth of war stamps. There, the American Legion Boys' Band played, and Ms. Lamour spoke to an enthralled crowd, many of whom were young people who had never seen

Dorothy Lamour. Life *magazine, July 7, 1941.*

a movie star before. The 7:30 p.m. appearance at the auditorium required the purchase of a war bond—the higher the denomination, the better the seat. When Ms. Lamour appeared, over three thousand people had jammed the old wooden hall to join in the patriotic festivities. The Dow Field Band played martial music, and city political and civic leaders sat on stage along with key officers from Dow Field. Ms. Lamour's rallying speech plus the mass induction of over forty young men into the navy highlighted this program.

Businesses encouraged their employees to purchase war stamps and bonds through payroll deduction plans and contests. The *Bangor Daily News* randomly photographed people downtown, published the picture and placed

a circle around one person in the picture. Known as "Watch for Your Photo," this contest awarded a two-dollar war stamp for the person who came into the office to identify himself or herself. The Bangor School Department promoted the sale of bonds and stamps in the schools and encouraged contests and competitions between schools. The school that sold the most bonds and stamps had the privilege of flying a "Minute Man" flag from the flagpole. The Fairmount School across from the army's Fairmount Terrace was the first school in the war to fly this flag. Schoolchildren also signed a pledge to "solemnly promise to continue to buy United States Savings Stamps and Bonds to the limit of my ability." Over the course of the war, the government promoted bonds and stamps sales through numbered war loan campaigns; the war's daily monetary costs were tremendous.

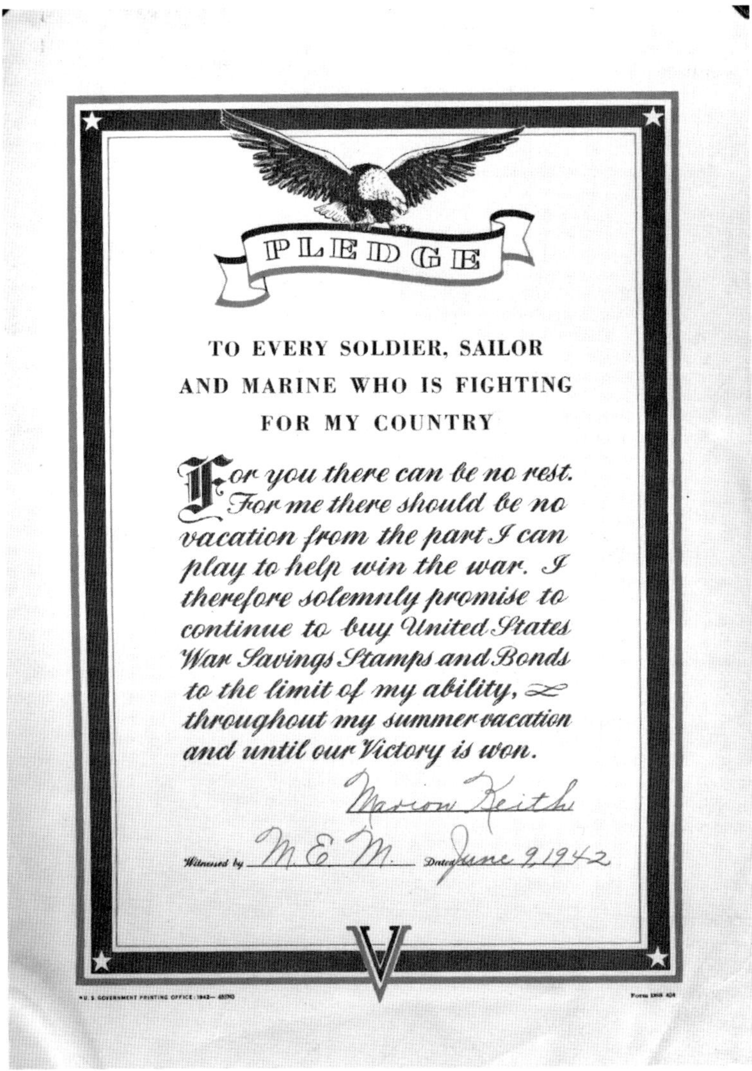

PLEDGE

TO EVERY SOLDIER, SAILOR AND MARINE WHO IS FIGHTING FOR MY COUNTRY

For you there can be no rest. For me there should be no vacation from the part I can play to help win the war. I therefore solemnly promise to continue to buy United States War Savings Stamps and Bonds to the limit of my ability, throughout my summer vacation and until our Victory is won.

Marion Keith

Witnessed by M.E.M. Dated June 9, 1942

A student's pledge to purchase war stamps and bonds. *Author's collection.*

Victory not only required vast expenditures of money, it also required the collection of scarce wartime resources. Part of this effort became known as scrap drives and engaged Bangoreans of all ages in individual and collective efforts. Even before Pearl Harbor, Bangoreans participated in scrap collections of precious metals, particularly aluminum. The American Legion, helped by newly arrived soldiers from the air base, set up and manned a receptacle in West Market Square. Here they collected pots, pans and cooking utensils. Later that summer, Boy Scouts took up the cause, collecting over 2,500 household items made of aluminum. Other children brought aluminum items to the Bijou Theater on Exchange Street; these served as their admission ticket. A huge pile of aluminum resulted, and the city needed a large truck to haul the collection to the railroad yard.

Soon after Pearl Harbor, the city appointed a salvage committee to oversee vital scrap drives. City council chairman Frank O. Youngs appealed to citizens to use this opportunity to clean house while helping the war cause. The country needed a variety of precious materials, rubber being one. Japanese forces overran rubber-rich areas of Southeast Asia, so this resource was in short supply across the nation. At low tide, Boy Scouts fished out discarded tires from the Kenduskeag Stream. The M. Lynch Company, locksmiths, began an "Old Keys to Build a Bomber" campaign. Keys contained brass, copper and nickel—valuable metal for wartime production. This unique program soon attracted a lot of attention among the public, who, in turn, riffled through drawers and cabinets for unused household and car keys. Schoolchildren in Bangor joined this popular drive. Students at the Fifth Street Junior High School turned in a heavy box containing over five thousand keys. Even college-aged students such as Allan Woodcock Jr., a student at Bowdoin College, contributed their private collections of keys. In Bangor, schools, both public and parochial, were centers for a large metal scrap drive on Monday, September 14, 1942. Increased war production reduced the nation's steel scrap inventory by 40 percent, so on this "Junk Day," students and teachers brought their scrap metal and rubber to school and collected donations from citizens who dropped off their junk.

The rationing program, introduced by the federal government in early 1942, brought the war's reality into the everyday lives of Bangoreans. Commodities and foodstuffs, which for years had been so plentiful, began to be in short supply as the country struggled to feed its military forces, its allies and its citizens and to supply the fuel needed to propel its mechanized military. The city established a local rationing board at federal government direction in order to monitor local compliance. Over the next few years, Bangor citizens came to know in real terms about the survival of the country—not so much about the survival of democracy as so eloquently spoken about by FDR, but the survival of their daily lives as they knew it. At first, the federal government announced a gasoline "curtailment" program because of the increase in sinkings of oil tankers by Nazi submarines along the eastern seaboard. Also, the government increasingly diverted oil tankers to supply needed fuel to hard-pressed England. A gasoline-rationing program for Bangor started by mid-May by evaluating people's fuel needs. Bangoreans registered for gasoline rationing at a local school from late afternoon to early evening from May 12 through May 14. Teachers acted as registrars and questioned over five thousand citizens as to their automobile usage, classifying their needs according to government standards. An individual using his or her vehicle purely for pleasure received an A classification while teachers initially classified others who used a vehicle to commute to work in one of three B categories. By July, the city had distributed a gas ration book to those who had registered. Each book was for a year and contained forty-eight coupons, each worth four gallons of gasoline. Those in category A received only one book. Each category had a limited entitlement of gasoline; citizens could appeal their classification to the Bangor Rationing Board. A similar system for sugar was already in place. Other domestic rationing programs followed. For the United States and its people, the "total war" was just underway; victory remained elusive.

6

ONE OF OURS

The sun struggled to shine through rain-laden clouds as flags fluttered in the clearing breeze. The Dow Field Band marched by in quick tempo playing "The U.S. Air Force." Bangoreans cheered and hummed along with the words, "Off we go into the wild blue yonder," as their neighbor soldiers went by followed by army trucks bristling with guns. It was Memorial Day 1942 and the first time the band made an appearance in its hometown. The air base had formed the band earlier that spring when twenty-eight new musical instruments arrived from the quartermaster's depot in Philadelphia. Technical Sergeant Erwin called for tryouts and readily found his musicians. Throughout the war, the air base band thrilled the people of Bangor in the many parades that followed.[52]

From the very first soldiers who had arrived at Union Station the previous spring to the end of the war, Bangoreans overwhelmingly welcomed their soldier guests, often referring to them as "Bangor's New Family." Mrs. Henry C. Knowlton of the newly formed Bangor Soldiers' Welfare Council set the tone when she called for Thanksgiving dinner invitations for air base personnel in early November 1941: "There is no more fitting way of our community to extend hospitality to the young men in service at our air base… we are hoping that many homes will take advantage of this opportunity of extending to these soldiers the welcome that we'd like to see given our Bangor boys in military service away from home."[53] Other successful citizen outreaches followed with invitations for enlisted men and officers to attend parties, dances and religious functions and to use area recreational facilities.

Dow Field Band. *Bangor Historical Society.*

Local resident Nick Fotis invited air base soldiers to use his dance pavilion and beach at Hermon Pond for swimming, boating and fishing. Later, the YMCA made its beautiful Camp Jordan facility at Branch Pond available for soldier recreation. Now soldiers, weather permitting, enjoyed the best Maine offered. As recently as 2013, Lyman Blackwell remembered the kindness of Bangoreans to airmen. He was simply passing through Dow Field as a B-17 crew member on his way to Europe when a bad snowstorm stranded him and his crew mates for a week over the Christmas 1944 holiday. Caring citizens sponsored a Christmas party for all of the crew at the YMCA, and when Blackwell returned to his temporary barracks, a gift waited for him on his bunk bed. The gift package contained a green tie with a note with holiday wishes from a Bangor elementary school girl.[54]

The army took measures as well to foster good community relations. The 43rd Bombardment Group's newsletter in its front-page article "Just a Moment…" set the standard for soldier behavior within the surrounding community: "The good soldier is always careful to be courteous and considerate toward civilians." Later, when soldiers arrived for duty at Dow Field, no matter how long, they all received a booklet titled *Dow Field and Surroundings*. The public relations office at the air base produced this helpful

Dow Field men swimming at Camp Jordan. *Bangor Historical Society.*

guide to acquaint the new soldier with Bangor. The local newspapers quickly provided copy space to enlighten their readers about their new neighbors. The *Bangor Daily News* in the early fall of 1941 carried a weekly news column titled "The Wind Sock." Here, the soldiers wrote about themselves and shared with Bangoreans what they could about their life at the air base. Soldiers described themselves as representing a wide variety of nationalities, classes and religions. They came from all parts of the country; some had college educations, some no formal education beyond eighth grade. They also described themselves physically as being, on average, five feet, eight inches tall, weighing 144 pounds, having a waist size of thirty-one inches and wearing a size-nine-and-a-half shoe and a seven-inch hat. The air base soldiers said that their one uniting factor was their common goal to defend the nation. After Pearl Harbor, the army discontinued this informative column, opting instead to publish its own weekly newspaper called the *Dow Field Observer*.

Bangor civic organizations often sought out base officers as speakers for weekly meetings, particularly the different commanding officers over time. This helped civic leaders stay informed about the activities at the base and also about how the city could be helpful to its soldier residents. At a May 1942 Rotary Club meeting, members queried guest speaker Colonel George E. Lovell Jr., third air base commander after Colonel Wells, about the war. Colonel Lovell responded cautiously but optimistically: "We'll win, of course, but it's going to be a long, hard job." He then commended the fine cooperation between the city and the air base. The Kiwanis Club, however, sought to learn more about the soldiers at the base by inviting them, in small groups, to its weekly meetings. Each of the members took on two soldiers as their personal guests, introduced them to the club and sought to get to know them through conversation about their lives prior to the army.

Musical entertainment was one avenue that helped Bangoreans learn about the troops at the air base. Many soldiers possessed capable musical talent, which they willingly shared with the public. At times, some soldiers performed classical violin and piano solos for city organizations; at other times, some soldiers filled positions with the Bangor Symphony Orchestra. Vocally talented soldiers performed renditions of contemporary popular music. In September 1942, WLBZ radio instituted a weekly radio broadcast from the base's theater called *Dow Field on the Air*, a show that featured a vocalist performing music to the accompaniment of the Dow Field Troubadours, a subgroup of the Dow Field Band. It was this group, in particular, and their performances of big band music at the municipal auditorium for the Army Emergency Relief campaigns that drew Bangoreans' attention. Open to the public, these benefit dances attracted hundreds to an evening of swing while raising money to support soldiers and their dependents caught in a financial emergency. As the war progressed and as soldiers rotated to new duty stations, new musical groups appeared. The Five Dow Field Hep Cats, Sergeant Diamond's Dow Field Aces, Dow Field Octet, Dow Field Ensemble and Sergeant Blinn's Dow Field Jive Bombers were but some of the successor musical ensembles.

Sports were another means by which Bangoreans came to know the soldiers at Dow Field. Many soldiers, prior to enlistment, were high school or college athletes. Once at the air base, soldiers naturally came together to participate in various sports. The first organized team even before Pearl Harbor was a football squad composed of men from the ordnance company who called themselves the Bangor Bobcats. They played the Augusta Cadets and other squads that fall. Once the weather became more moderate that next spring, soldiers organized a baseball team. Now calling themselves the Dow Field Bombers, the baseball team took on local town teams such as Dexter, Old Town, Thomaston and the Bangor

Sergeant Blinn performing. *Bangor Historical Society.*

Bears. They played, at times, against impromptu teams also from the base at Hayford's Field, to the delight of watching sports-minded Bangoreans. The games with the Brewer Red Sox at the Brewer Athletic Field were always crowd pleasers. Playoffs with teams from other area army air forces bases developed into competitive regional playoffs. In July 1943, the Bombers met the Colby Cadets in front of more than three thousand spectators at the college's Woodman Stadium for what was billed as the Army Championship of Maine. The Cadets stopped the Bombers in a close game, winning the championship 2–1. It was in basketball, though, that the Dow Field athletes gained their greatest notoriety. Sticking with the successful moniker first adopted by the baseball team, the Dow Field Bombers racked up basketball victories playing other service groups until local sportswriters hailed them as "number one." They also played and soundly defeated local teams such as the Ellsworth Red Wings on the courts of their new base gymnasium. In the winter of 1945, the Bombers flew to Grenier Field in Manchester, New Hampshire, to participate in the North Atlantic Division Tournament of the Air Transport Command. There, they defeated LaGuardia Field in an overtime game 36–34. In the championship game, the Bombers took on Presque Isle but were trounced in a fast-paced game that thrilled spectators. And later in March, the Bombers took on the locally strong basketball team Leen's Electronics to win a fifteen-game YMCA tournament. Base leadership encouraged participation in sports and made resources and equipment readily available with a new base gymnasium that opened in September 1943. Base leadership also encouraged competitive boxing at the base. Major John Ballerino, referee of on-base boxing matches, called boxing a "manly art…a good soldier sport." For the military coaches, though, recruiting a squad posed problems. The 1944 baseball team had only three of 1943's

The gymnasium at the base opened in September 1943. *Bangor Historical Society.*

nine players; the other players had rotated to new wartime assignments. This was true for all organized athletics, as the war came first.

The local USO represented Bangor's predominant effort to extend hometown hospitality to Dow Field soldiers. The USO on West Broadway offered leisure activities daily and scheduled evening programs. Annette McCarthy and other young Bangor women served as USO hostesses, conducted weekly quiz games and "topsy turvy" scavenger hunts and showed movies. They danced with soldiers at weekly dances at the Roseland Ballroom to the music of Norman Lambert's Orchestra. In warmer weather, soldiers and hostesses played volleyball, badminton, tether ball and croquet on the spacious lawns. By the fall of 1942, however, "the home away from home" on West Broadway was too small for the base's burgeoning soldier population. Bangor took action, and Mrs. Gordon D. Briggs of the local USO advisory committee announced that the larger Tarratine Club on Park Street in downtown Bangor was the new USO Club beginning in 1943. Also that fall, the USO opened a club on Columbia Street in the former GAR building for the growing number of African American soldiers stationed at Dow Field. The army air forces, at that time, remained a segregated military service; even on base, African American soldiers had their own service club building apart from white servicemen.

The new USO was now open twenty-four hours a day. The larger, less-staid facility allowed for on-premises dances and jitterbug contests, a real hit with soldiers. Musicals featuring local and air base talent had space to perform. "Spirit of the Air Corps" dances welcomed new airmen to Bangor, and jam sessions with Victrola music were popular. The added space even allowed an occasional fashion show with WAACs from the base among the models displaying the latest haute couture on loan from local merchants. The Bangor USO, with funding from its supporting agencies of the Young Men's Christian Association, National Catholic Community Service, Salvation Army, Young Women's Christian Association, Jewish Welfare Board and National Travelers Aid Association, contributed significantly to making the Bangor airman one of our own.

7
OFF THEY GO

Light northwest winds whipped wisps of snow across the east–west runway as A-29s of the 92nd Reconnaissance Squadron landed at Dow Field. It was Wednesday, February 4, 1942. The 43rd Bombardment Group with its three squadrons and the attached 13th Reconnaissance Squadron had left just days earlier for the Pacific war zone. Its soldiers who came to know Bangor as home were now winged warriors anxious to engage the enemy. Some airmen never returned. Bangoreans followed their story with hometown interest when the army made news available. The 92nd continued the submarine patrol begun by the 19th Reconnaissance Squadron. Colonel Harold R. Wells took command of the air base for a few weeks after Colonel Connell left for Washington and before Colonel George E. Lovell Jr., the new base commander, arrived in Bangor.[55]

The 2,800-man air base was a whirlwind of activity those first few months of the war. The army rotated various units stationed there elsewhere. The 8th Air Force Base Group, an administrative and base maintenance unit and one of the first to arrive at the new Bangor air base the previous summer, left to help set up new air bases overseas. Other units soon followed as the War Department struggled to meet the materiel and personnel demands of a two-front war. Colonel Lovell opened the base for public inspection on Army Day, Monday, April 6, an unusual move since it was wartime. The base's 1st Air Force Headquarters at Mitchel Field authorized the open house but placed the base on "alert." All troops stood by at their duty stations ready for any battle order. More than 5,000 citizens came by car, foot, bus and bicycle to view parts of the base on tour from 2:00 to 5:00 p.m. Visitors viewed exhibits set up near the Hammond Street gate that included bombs, machine guns, field pieces and medical and chemical warfare displays. Selected soldiers guided tours through the cantonment area, past newly constructed storehouses and up the hill to the east, where the expansive base hospital was located. From there, observant Bangoreans looked to the north over to Fuller Road and saw acres of empty farmland that still ran along Union Street. The government had its eye on this land, too, as purchase proceedings had just started days earlier. Seven hundred acres were involved; the War Department needed this space as part of its plan for victory. The arrival in late December of Company C of the 36th Engineers gave a hint.

The first of the heavy bombardment groups appeared by May and used Dow Field as training and staging for the war in Europe. The 97th Bombardment Group (Heavy) was among the first of several to leave from Dow Field for England after a brief period of training in long-range navigation.[56] Using newly constructed air bases in remote regions of the North Atlantic, the B-17s of the group flew in an arched circuit called the Great Circle Route, first to Goose Bay, Labrador; on to Gander, Newfoundland, next; then to Nararssuak, Greenland (Bluie West I); on to Meeks Field, Iceland; and finally into Preswick, Scotland, before dispersal to newly established airdromes in eastern England. At each stop on this dangerous route, air base crews refueled the aircraft, provided needed servicing, fed the airmen and sent them on their way. The 1st Fighter Group, briefly stationed at Dow Field, flying the twin-engine P38, accompanied the bombers of the 97th. This historic flight of warplanes to Europe was the first such flight and proved the viability of this route to the battlefields across the Atlantic to War Department planners.[57] The 97th was the first 8th Air Forces heavy bombardment group to carry out a mission against Hitler's Festung Europa. On August 17, the 97th took off from its English air base to bomb a railroad yard at Rouen, France.[58]

In addition to the 97th, other bombardment groups gathered at Dow Field and then left for England. Among these were the 92nd, the 93rd and the 303rd.[59] The 91st also left from the Bangor air base and included what would become the most famous of all World War II bombers, *Memphis Belle*. The Ferry Command, later succeeded by the Air Transport Command, flew in brand-new B-17s fresh from the factories to Dow Field. That summer of 1942, Brigadier General B.F. Miles was at Dow Field to review the ferrying operations with the new base commander, Colonel Francis B. Valentine.[60] Colonel Valentine, previously commander of the departed 43rd

Bombardment Group, returned to assume base command after the departure of Colonel Lovell. Typically, airmen arrived by train at Union Station, where base transportation met them. James Stanley recalled how busy Union Station was during the war with the arrival and departure of servicemen and women.[61] Once at the base, aircrews were housed and trained until departure. Officers at times were able to hook a ride with an army airplane destined for Bangor. This was the case with First Lieutenant Robert K. Morgan, pilot of the *Memphis Belle*. The new bomber sitting on the tarmac was a B-17 F with the tail number 4485 and was the latest model of many variations of the B-17, each later variation incorporating improvements as a result of battle experience. Morgan recalled seeing his bomber for the first time: "I walked out to where she was parked…the first chance I got and gave her the once-over. It was love at first sight…Olive-drab, covered partly with camouflage paint, her several turrets bristling with machine gun barrels, she seemed the perfect combination of delicate grace and warlike toughness."[62] Air forces tradition allowed for crews to name their aircraft and to paint appropriate caricatures on the nose section of the plane. For Morgan's crew, arriving at a democratic consensus for the name of their new bomber was problematic. Ten strongly held ideas, one for each of the ten crew members, prevented an agreement. Morgan wanted the aircraft named after his girlfriend Margaret Polk of Memphis, Tennessee, so he decided to break this logjam in an unconventional way. He reasoned if he could get another vote for his idea from another member of the crew, then that would be the selected name. He targeted his tail gunner, "a stocky red-haired fellow from Yonkers named John Quinlan." Morgan invited Quinlan to have a few beers at a local establishment off base. There, Morgan plied Quinlan with "cold ones" until Quinlan agreed with Morgan's name suggestion and pledged his vote at the next crew meeting. Quinlan was true to his word, and Morgan's name, *Memphis Belle*, received the most votes. Squadron artist Corporal Tony Starcer painted the later-to-become-famous nose art adapted from *Esquire Magazine*.[63]

The 8th Air Force implemented its policy of precision daylight bombing from the very beginning of its bombing campaign as begun by the 97th. This approach, it was thought, reduced innocent civilian casualties by targeting only war-making industries and facilities. The British had long abandoned this approach in favor of massive nighttime "terror" bombing. The American aircrews, however, paid the price, as they were viciously shot from the skies by Luftwaffe pilots. As an incentive and morale booster for these crews, officials promised to rotate them back to the United States if they successfully completed twenty-five bomb missions. Chances of this

Union Railroad Station. *Author's collection.*

The crew of the *Memphis Belle*. Lieutenant Robert Morgan is fifth from the left. *National Museum of the U.S. Air Force.*

really happening were one in five. The *Memphis Belle* was lucky and was the first recognized bomber to meet this number in June 1943. *Memphis Belle* and its crew returned home for a war bond tour. Hollywood producer Willy Wyler made a short film about this achievement, and when FDR viewed it, the president told Wyler to show the film in every theater in the country.[64] And it all started at Dow Field.

The civilian workforce at Dow Field grew in importance as the war effort progressed. Bangoreans applied through Civil Service as positions became available; some positions required competitive examinations. Particularly crucial were aircraft mechanics, sheet metal workers and electrical specialists needed to make repairs or modifications to aircraft being ferried through the base.[65] The U.S. Civil Service Commission in early fall 1942 established the State of Maine Aircraft School at the Brewer Armory to train aircraft mechanics, an urgent need. Twelve-week courses provided basic mechanical instruction, as well as some instruction in specialized aircraft maintenance. Graduates then took jobs at the aircraft maintenance sub-depot (a service unit) at the air base and none

A civilian worker explains his work to an airbase officer. A WAAC looks on. *Bangor Historical Society.*

Civilian workers on a quartermaster warehouse loading dock at Dow Field. *Bangor Historical Society.*

too soon; the army's 441st Service Squadron left for overseas in November. Civilians now performed all mechanical work on aircraft in the base's shops.[66] These Bangorean workers at the base found a cohesiveness among themselves and formed the Sub-Depot Employees Association that fall; they sponsored social functions and encouraged war bond sales. Like their fellow workers elsewhere in Bangor, they worked for victory.

With the exception of hearing the army aircraft at the base,[67] few Bangoreans realized the level of activity there. They took pride in their local air base, first built for defense but now working for victory. They noted with interest the construction by the army corps of engineers of an airport with two four-thousand-foot runways in nearby Winterport that could be used by base aircraft if need be. But they had their own daily wartime lives to contend with. Life in Bangor that summer took on a subdued tone. The city council banned fireworks, so only a few cap pistols were heard that Fourth of July. W.H. Hinman, organizer of the Bangor Fair, announced its cancellation for the summer, saying, "There can be but one job for all of us—win this war." Civil defense tests continued. On August 28, air sirens sounded at 2:55

p.m., sending more than three thousand Bangoreans scurrying to downtown shelters all within three minutes. Local defense officials coordinated this exercise with the army's First Service Command in Boston and the Maine National Guard. Interestingly, the exercise included a theoretical attack on Dow Field. Over five hundred wardens were on duty in Bangor that summer and continued to work frequently with citizens to help them conform to blackout standards. New blackout regulations particularly governed the flow of traffic. When officials turned off the streetlights, thereby signaling a "red alert," all traffic pulled over and stopped. During these tests, wardens let only cars with headlight shades move if necessary. In the kitchens of Bangor, housewives learned to bake with less sugar as that commodity, the first of many, was now strictly rationed. And now, chairman of the rationing board Thomas N. Curran reminded his fellow citizens to renew their gas rationing books on October 21. Fuel oil users could register at the high school or at one of the two junior highs for their 1943 winter allotment of heating oil beginning on Monday, October 26.

Senator Harry S. Truman from Missouri and two other senators, all members of the noted Senate watchdog committee on government defense spending, briefly stopped at Dow Field on August 20 as part of a statewide air base inspection tour. As the Beechcraft biplane rolled to a stop, Colonel Lovell and Major General Sherman Miles of the 1st Air Force Service Command were there to greet Truman, who was accompanied by Maine's own Senator Ralph O. Brewster and West Virgina's Senator Harley M. Kilgore. The group met in the new headquarters building and then toured the air base. Truman saw some of the fifty-seven new buildings under construction by the Cunningham Company. He also saw that personnel had painted all of the base's original white buildings olive drab. Even the base's checkered standpipe conformed to the wartime color scheme. When asked by reporters to comment on what he saw, Truman replied that he was "very much impressed" with the progress of the expanding air base. City manager Fred D. Farnsworth wasn't quite so happy; he was alarmed at the damage to nearby city roads caused by continuing construction. Army corps of engineers crews were cutting ditches across parts of Fuller Road to the north near newly acquired land while on the south, corps equipment was damaging sections of Odlin Road from Hammond Street to where they were constructing a new service road to an ordnance depot in nearby Hampden. In each case, Farnsworth deemed the roads impassable and a danger to the public but diplomatically demurred from taking any legal action to resolve the problem in the interests of wartime support.

As Bangoreans traveled about town that fall, they noticed fifty-one street scrap bins placed at key locations. These signaled a new scrap drive. Organizers once again encouraged schoolchildren to participate. But a controversy soon arose when some well-meaning citizens suggested that historic cannons placed about the city in various parks be given up to the scrap drive. These war relics contained many pounds of precious metal now needed to wage the current conflict. The *Bangor Daily News* supported this initiative and sought to gain Bangoreans' support when it printed ballots in its early October issues that encouraged its readers to vote as "I favor" or "I do not favor" scrapping the old war relics. The cannons in question were from different periods in Bangor's history. Several scattered throughout the city were from the Civil War era.

One had been hauled up in 1885 from the floor of Bangor harbor by James Fennell, captain of the dredger *Bothfield*. This relic was thought to be from the 1779 Penobscot expedition when American Revolutionaries, including Paul Revere, scuttled their fleet in Penobscot Bay all the way up to the mouth of the Kenduskeag Stream to keep their ships from being captured by the British. Another interesting war relic was a six-thousand-pound Spanish cannon from the Spanish-American War that graced downtown's Norumbega Mall. The Spanish mined the copper and brass from Mexico and then fabricated the cannon in Spain to stand guard on the fort overlooking Havana Harbor. This cannon found its way after the Spanish-American War to Bangor through the efforts of then congressman from the Third District Charles A. Boutelle. Many citizens thought this Spanish cannon in particular was a scrap-drive prize. Even Boutelle's three daughters weighed in and encouraged its scrapping, saying that their father would want this done. Reverend Aubrey Winsor, pastor of the Essex Street Baptist Church, expressed his sentiment on the debate in rhythmic verse:

> *I am perfectly willing to be placed on the spot, and hit the iron while it is hot. This is no time for wistful thinking, but practical performance. These cannon were made for war. Like a lot of folks they have been ornaments long enough—put them into the service for which they were created. At this hour mere sentiment is silly, senseless, and a sin. The will to win through service and sacrifice must now begin. After the war is won, there will be cannon, for everyone. Let no partiality be shown—use them to make the Nazi and Nips moan, for they are the ones who have sown, as history will tell—the seeds of Hate, Horror, and Hell. We need to ask and answer one question in this All-Out War. Are our daughters and sons less precious than ornamental cannon?*[58]

The Spanish cannon still sits at the State Street side of Norumbega Parkway. *Author's collection.*

By mid-October, the *Bangor Daily News* reported that the ratio of Bangoreans supporting the scrapping of the cannons was sixteen to one. Fortunately, the city council disagreed, reserving this move only for the time when all other scrap metal, including junked autos, was exhausted. Even so, citizens did collect over one million pounds of scrap metal that fall. And Dow Field contributed to the nation's need for scrap metal when in November it salvaged eight tons of aluminum from the wrecked bomber in Springfield.

The United States continued to try to find its footing in the two-front war. In May 1942, the navy foiled a Japanese advance on Australia in the Battle of the Coral Sea and won a decisive victory over the Japanese in the Battle of Midway a month later. The U.S. Marines landed on Guadalcanal in early August and started their bloody six-month campaign to take that island back for the Allies. Here, the Americans learned firsthand about the tough and stubborn fighting credo of the Japanese warrior. On the other side of the globe, the United States joined with the British to launch an attack on French North Africa due much to the insistence of Stalin to put pressure elsewhere on Nazi forces. Dubbed "Torch," this campaign

Young Bangorean Donald Stewart (center) leaves from Union Station for war. *Elizabeth Crowley collection.*

introduced the American foot soldier to the fierce fighting to come in Europe.[69] In Bangor, over six hundred young men between the ages of eighteen and twenty registered for selective service. A change in the law lowered the eligible age for induction from twenty-one. More and more young men left Union Station either as volunteers or as inductees; this trend only continued to grow as the war progressed.

As temperatures dropped and snow piled up, the level of war activity at Dow Field diminished significantly over the 1942–43 winter months. The army air forces had not yet reduced the hazards of flying for its crews and crafts in ferocious winter weather over a turbulent North Atlantic. However, selected adventurous aircrews in specially equipped weather planes flew out into this region during the region's worst weather, gathering data helpful for navigation and weather forecasting.[70] The bombers so desperately needed in England needed to fly to Europe no matter the time of year. Reorganization of units filled up this quiet time at Dow Field until the big push began with the arrival of better weather.

8
DOING THEIR PART

The great chamber doors flew open with a thud against the stops. Out hastened a diminutive bespectacled lady one step ahead of a maddened crowd. Down the arched hallway she flew while flashbulbs popped with lightning-like glare and the din of swelling thunder reverberated off marbled floors and vaulted ceilings. The human storm chased her until she chanced by an empty phone booth along the corridor, into which she flew and slammed the bi-fold doors shut, seeking safety and silence. Jeanette Rankin, representative from Montana and the first woman ever to serve in Congress, voted "no" in the House of Representatives' December 8 resolution to go to war with Japan. Hers was the only negative vote in the entire Congress. She reasoned, "As a woman, I cannot go to war, and I refuse to send anyone else."[71] Miss Rankin's courageous vote delivered in a milieu of revenge and reprisal against America's Asian enemy focused the country's attention on what women could do in a new war.

Forbidden by national law to fight, women nevertheless mobilized for war. And they found a way to join the army when President Roosevelt signed the Women's Auxiliary Army Corps (WAACs) into law on May 16, 1942. Formed to assist the army to successfully execute the war in noncombat ways, the army's organized women grew in number and in importance as the war progressed.

In Bangor, the first group of four WAACs arrived in mid-October 1942 after completion of their basic training in Des Moines, Iowa. Two immediately took positions at the filter center, relieving hard-pressed civilian volunteers from the army's twenty-four-hour, seven-days-a-week command center for enemy aircraft monitoring. The other two joined the army's recruiting station on Central Street.[72] More soon followed.

The WAACs at the army's recruitment office immediately began a campaign to recruit women between the ages of twenty-one and forty-five for army service. In previous wars, women had always found ways to support the soldiers and sailors, but enlisting for military service in those days was a novel idea. Lieutenants Nina E. Donahue and Arlene B. Goodridge spoke to civic groups that fall about the role of the WAACs in the new war. Bangor women volunteered to help them by assisting in the interview process, and a late November bond drive with the campaign title "Women for War Week" helped to focus the community's attention on ways women supported America's fighting efforts. By mid-December, eight area women had enlisted and taken the Oath of Loyalty at the WAACs' own recruiting office on Columbia Street.

A week before Christmas, a detachment of 103 WAACs arrived at Union Station eager to support the community's war effort; they were initially housed at city hotels until the city determined permanent downtown lodging. One site looked at by the city for housing the WAACs was the Coe Estate on Court Street, a collection of buildings used for school purposes. Meanwhile, the new WAACs joined other WAACs already at the filter center. Of course, women-starved soldiers at Dow Field noticed this new group and vice versa. The WAACs sponsored a Christmas Day party and invited selected Dow Field soldiers. The all-day party went from nine o'clock in the morning until eleven-thirty that evening. Dow soldiers described the affair: "We think it was one of the longest Christmas parties in history, and one of the best."[73] Other social gatherings followed.

WAAC recruitment proceeded at a brisk pace. By late January, twelve new recruits had left for basic at Fort Devens, Massachusetts. Sixteen women left for WAAC training in February, but WAAC recruiters hoped for more. Recruiters found convincing conservative Maine women about army life challenging. A massive WAAC recruiting campaign that spring organized out of the WAACs' Bangor recruiting station and part of a national effort aspired to increase recruitment. Bangor hosted on April 19 the WAAC "Caravan," which included performances by a forty-eight-piece symphony orchestra, patriotic dramatic and musical acts and a buffet dinner. This special day started with a parade from Pickering Square led by the Dow Field Band that stopped at the USO on Park Street for a special meal and then ended at city hall auditorium for the army show that evening. The program wanted to recruit fifty new WAACs but only managed to sign up six, who left for training the next week as the "Queen City Platoon." More followed later in the spring. By early summer, a new WAAC recruitment campaign was in place in Bangor. Called the Junior WAAC Recruiters Campaign, this uniquely Maine program sought to enroll girls between the ages of twelve and eighteen who themselves were too young to join but who could encourage their older sister(s) to join the WAACs. Local girls easily joined by filling out a newspaper coupon worded "I Want to Be a Junior WAAC Recruiter" and sent it in to the recruiting office on Columbia Street.

Oddly, that spring, the detachment of WAACs who had arrived just before Christmas left Bangor on March 23 from Union Station in two special train cars. Many Bangoreans turned out to see them off as their presence in the downtown and their winning ways had gained the affection of many citizens. Saddened soldiers from Dow Field drove trucks full of their baggage that they had picked up from the WAACs' quarters at the Penobscot Exchange Hotel and the Bangor House. WAACs from the Bangor recruiting station and civilians from the filter center wished them well as they boarded the train dressed in their smart khaki uniforms. Their destination was secret, but they were needed elsewhere. The WAACs were off to do what they could for their country.

The morale of the Dow Field soldiers soon picked up when the 91st WAAC Post Headquarters Company arrived on base on April 10, 1943. By this time, military commanders recognized what the army's women could do on base to help the war effort. Colonel Francis Valentine was no exception; he quickly put the WAAC company to work in clerical, communications, weather and supply positions. Third Officer Iva L. Culbertson headed the detachment. The WAAC barracks, mess hall and headquarters building occupied space on the hill to the east of the main cantonment; the soldiers knew the area as WAAC Hill.[74] Here, they joined 150,000 other WAACs across the nation by filling vital noncombat roles; their work released soldiers for combat duty.

The Dow soldiers wondered if their WAACs had a "pin-up boy" just as they had their pin-up girls. The base's paper, the *Observer*, conducted a survey late that spring and published the answer to that question in its June 14, 1943 issue. WAACs responded with an overwhelming consensus among them that they did not need a pin-up boy, as "we need no escape mechanisms and don't believe in anything as silly as pin-up boys." A few WAAC respondents, though, admitted that they had a pin-up boy: four had Clark Gable, two had Bob Hope and one each had Peter Lorre, Tyrone Power, Walter Pidgeon and Mickey Mouse.

WAACs on WAAC Hill. *Bangor Public Library.*

That summer, President Roosevelt signed legislation that changed the status of the WAACs from an auxiliary to an actual part of the army, which entitled them to all the rights and privileges that enlisted men enjoyed. Now known as the Women's Army Corps, or WACs, the women proved themselves to any skeptic. A special ceremony at the base in August officially recognized this recent organizational change. Colonel Valentine valued the work of the WACs at the base, now redesignated the 707th Post WAC Headquarters Company, and said he could use 150 more of them if available. And the soldiers, as if not to miss a beat, held a special welcome party that fall for the purpose of "having WACs and GIs meet."[75] And none too soon, for on November 26, the army, constantly reorganizing and reshuffling itself in a fast-moving war, deactivated the WAC company and sent them elsewhere; by December, all WACs had left Dow Field.

Other women filled crucial roles at Dow Field as well. In January 1943, Colonel Valentine appointed Mrs. Madeline Shaw, formerly at Fort Devens, as the base hostess or activities director. Her friendly smile and natural charm made her a favorite among Dow Field soldiers. She organized an available building into an inviting recreational hall complete with jukebox, games, card tables and radio. She organized weekly dances in a nearby base building and maintained a "date" list for officers and enlisted men. Almost four hundred young Bangorean women composed the list, all of whom were eager to meet Dow soldiers. She also kept a current listing of available housing in Bangor for married soldiers, a challenging task as local housing was in short supply during the war. Colonel Valentine appointed Mrs. Alyce Connor about this same time as base librarian. Formerly with the Bangor Public Library, Mrs. Connor built a library from scratch, collecting and cataloguing books ranging from light fiction to technical manuals. She instituted music nights that featured selected classical recordings. And like Mrs. Shaw, homesick soldiers quickly found Alyce Connor with her warm-hearted personality someone they easily shared their concerns with besides one of the chaplains. Many times, she wrote letters home for soldiers who found it hard to do so. The motherly team of Madeline Shaw and Alyce Connor helped the soldiers feel at home on the base.[76]

The volunteer women of the American Red Cross were a constant presence at the base and provided a cornucopia of humanitarian services to the airmen there. The Gray Ladies, so called because of the color of their uniforms, served in the base's sprawling four-ward hospital helping wounded and ill soldiers heal by increasing their human contact, working with them in arts and crafts projects, assisting them in writing letters home, stimulating their senses with lively conversation, playing games and challenging their intellect through reading. By early 1944, the Gray Ladies who were inducted after training in a fall 1942 ceremony at the Hebrew Community Center had served over six thousand volunteer hours at the base hospital. Young Red Cross–trained nurses' aides each volunteered four hours weekly and assisted the hospital's medical staff with routine medical procedures and patient care. The Red Cross's Motor Corps provided the transportation service for Red Cross canteen workers who met each incoming aircrew as they stopped at Dow Field on their way to the European Theater of Operations. These Bangor volunteer women had an assigned day of the week; upon receiving a phone call, they picked up the necessary supplies and their assigned canteen workers and then traveled to the base. The canteen workers gladly offered coffee and doughnuts to just-landed flyers and often were thanked by the airmen's simple words: "Glad to, Mom."

Eight full-time nurses at the hospital oversaw the day-to-day convalescence of patients. A chief nurse, in conjunction with the base surgeon, managed patient care. Nurses assisted the surgeon during surgery in one of the two hospital operating rooms. First Lieutenant Mary B. Robinson helped to

Above: A Gray Lady reads to a wounded soldier at Dow Field Hospital. *Bangor Public Library.*

Right: Nurse's aide at Dow Field Hospital. *Bangor Public Library.*

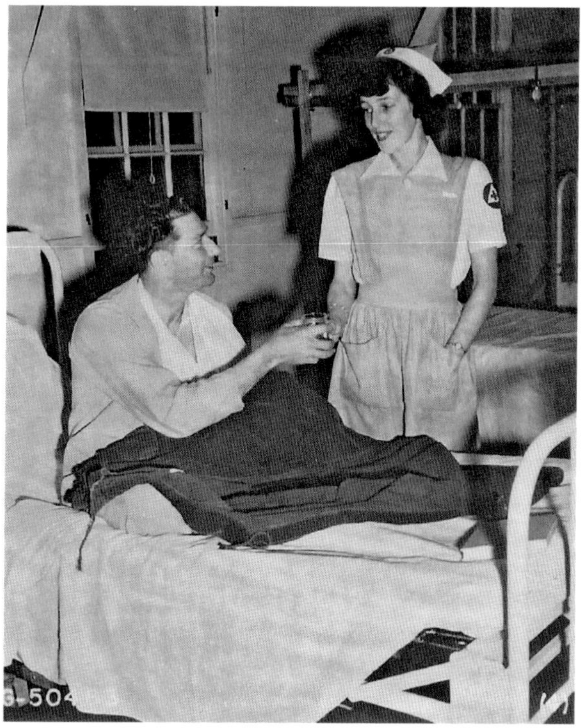

An army nurse (eleventh from left) amid wounded soldiers at Dow Field Hospital. *Bangor Public Library.*

The telephone center at Dow Field. *Bangor Public Library.*

open the hospital in July 1941 as chief nurse.[77] First Lieutenant Ruth E. Farrar later succeeded her.

In some cases, other civilian women filled positions critical to the military function of the base. This was true for the elaborate telephone center staffed by female telephone operators supervised by the very capable Kathleen Muir. Telephone operators needed to know every assigned position on the base and its extension number. The constantly flashing lights of the switchboard at times were unnerving and stressful, but calm people with calm voices managed this complicated function. For the officers, the center provided a link to headquarters and changing command orders in an evolving war; for the soldiers, the center provided a link to family and home.

First Lieutenant Madeline Proctor, graduate of Radcliffe College, reported to Dow Field in mid-July 1944. She, along with six other WACs, was part of the first contingent in a new WAC detachment to be based at the air base in almost a year. By September, the full complement of sixty WACs was in place on WAC Hill with Proctor in charge. The female soldiers filled driving positions in the motor pool and clerical positions in various

A Dow Field WAC updating information. *Bangor Public Library.*

Dow Field WACs and GIs out for a walk on base. *Bangor Public Library.*

base offices, and several enrolled in an on-base mechanics course. Colonel Jensen endorsed the WACs' return when he said, "The Army…needs more of these efficient soldiers in skirts." The soldiers were ecstatic and put on a parade in their honor. Now army men and women at Dow Field worked together for victory. The big push was on.

9

THE BIG PUSH

"Now, Ladies and Gentlemen, from the Bangor Opera House in Bangor, Maine, we bring you a comedian you'll get a big bang out of—Jack Benny," went Don Wilson's booming opening line. After some banter back and forth between Benny and Wilson, the popular comedian continued with, "Everybody's so nice up here. You know, Don, I'll never forget that reception at the station when we arrived. They had tanks and jeeps, sleighs, soldiers and Indians."[78] In fact, Jack Benny's arrival in the Queen City the day before his Sunday evening broadcast from the Bangor Opera House was quite a show. As his train pulled into Union Station around noon that Saturday, Bangoreans surged ahead to get a closer look at someone famous. With him were his regulars: Don Wilson, Dennis Day, Eddie "Rochester" Anderson, bandleader Abe Lyman and his wife, Mary Livingstone. The total troupe numbered thirty-nine. They were in Bangor to put on a show for the soldiers of Dow Field through the efforts of the local NBC radio affiliate, WLBZ. Despite the cold, the crowd cheered and clapped; the Dow Field Band played while Benny and his wife climbed into a small sleigh. Rochester climbed in, too, and took the reins, much to the delight of onlookers. With a snap of the whip, Rochester urged the young mare ahead, and the sleigh moved forward, its runners screeching along the dry pavement as a recent warm spell had melted any residual ice. The comedians followed the Dow Band, three turret tanks and jeeps jammed with soldiers from the base. At State Street, the impromptu parade took a sharp left, crossed the Kenduskeag bridge and then went left up the gradually sloping Main Street. All along the way, Bangoreans pressed forward as the parade went by. Chief Crowley and his police worked to keep the enthusiastic well-wishers at bay. At the WLBZ studio, the parade stopped, and Benny, Mary and Rochester got out of the sleigh and mounted the steps of the studio, where Princess Watawasco of the Penobscots waited. She gave Benny an Indian war club and a Maine guide shirt. Then the procession continued up to the Bangor House, where a welcoming banquet awaited and the guests of honor stayed overnight.[79]

Bangoreans lined the street again Sunday evening, this time in front of the Bangor Opera House, where Benny and his cast were to broadcast live in the nationwide weekly radio show. The broadcast, full of hilarity and good-natured humor, went on without a problem and toward the end featured the playing of the Maine "Stein Song" by Abe Lyman's Orchestra. The pleased audience of soldiers and guests joined in by singing the lyrics. Benny and cast performed a show before the 7:00 p.m. broadcast and then again afterward for 1,500 troops, who jammed the theater. Just before 9:00 p.m., this first audience left to allow soldiers waiting outside to come in for a repeat performance, and Benny and cast put on another show for

From left to right: Dennis Day (second), Mary Livingstone (fourth), Abe Lyman (fifth), Jack Benny (sixth), Don Wilson (eighth) and Rochester (ninth). *Richard R. Shaw.*

the second capacity audience. While only soldiers were admitted into the theater, Bangoreans were there as support and to be part of something big. Benny's visit to Bangor brought a brief interlude to people living through a glum season full of glum war news.

The United States had been at war a full year. While 1942 had some limited American victories, the outcome of the war at the beginning of 1943 remained uncertain. Nazi Germany, intact and strong, along with ally Fascist Italy, remained determined; Japanese forces dug in. Much hard fighting by the United States and its allies lay ahead. FDR, forever the optimist, called for the "unconditional surrender" of democracy's enemies at the Casablanca Conference in late January.

For Bangoreans and their soldier family, the war was real day by day. Bangoreans continued to feel the daily effects of domestic rationing. The four gallons per week did not go far in automobiles that averaged fifteen miles per gallon, so ridership on public transportation increased. But then the bus company announced a curtailed schedule that spring due to a shortage of gasoline. In addition to shoes, sugar, film, fuel oil and gasoline, another commodity the government added to the list that spring was meat. Little meat was available in the markets by the end of March. Bangor housewives were forced to adjust what they fed their families. The local restaurants the previous fall had seen this shortage coming and instituted a meatless day on their menus. This initiative by local businessmen was typical of the patriotic support found in Bangor. Throughout the war, retailers decorated their storefronts with displays supporting the war effort. A successful "Heroes Parade," sponsored in part by downtown merchants that previous July, drew thousands of spectators.

During that spring of 1943, Bangoreans witnessed an increasing number of their young men leave for military service. The induction center, now on Columbia Street, was hard pressed because of space to keep up with the number of draftees. By the end of May, officials moved this center to the more commodious Brewer Municipal Auditorium. Military recruiting remained active; recruiters frequently scheduled qualifying tests for potential officers. The navy's recruiters located in the old federal building sought fifty recruits that spring to serve on a new navy frigate to be named USS *Bangor* being built in the American Shipbuilding Corps yard in Loraine, Ohio. This novel effort resulted in what recruiters called the Bangor Platoon. The fifty young men, many of whom were just seventeen years old, joined en masse in an August ceremony presided over by Representative Frank Fellows, Maine's Third District congressman. Officials held the ceremony in Davenport Park,

Freese's Department Store wartime window display. *Richard R. Shaw.*

site of the USS *Maine* Memorial. Then the platoon marched off to the railroad station. On their way, the young boys noticed the many servicemen and women who plied the streets of Bangor that summer. Even the Coast Guard stationed men in Bangor to protect the city's valuable waterfront resources. Now, the Bangor Platoon was off to do its part in the global war.

The soldiers at Dow Field also observed a dramatic increase in wartime activity that spring. In early April, the first element of the 924th Engineer Regiment Aviation arrived and occupied the newly completed north side of the base near Union Street. By July, the full complement was here and reorganized itself into Headquarters and Service, 1905th, 1906th and 1913th Engineer Aviation Battalions. Bangoreans first saw these engineers in the Memorial Day parade. While they did not stay long in Bangor, their presence at the air base presaged a vital War Department strategy for winning the war in Europe and in the Far East. Aviation engineers were responsible for constructing the needed battlefront facilities to press the air attack on the enemy and advance into held territory. Much of what the engineers built were landing strips for fighters and bombers in remote Pacific jungles or in continental Europe. They also constructed roads, bridges, gun emplacements and water and sewer systems. Many times they worked under combat conditions. While at Dow Field, members of the 924th used their time to train and prepare for battlefront assignment.

They spent much of their "practice" time expanding the length of the Dow Field runways from 5,000 to 7,000 feet, making them some of the longest in the AAF. They also built a 2,500-foot runway for medium bombers at Pickerel Pond in Greenfield thirty miles northeast of Bangor.[80] There, in 1941, the government purchased between six thousand and seven thousand acres from former Penobscot County sheriff Orman B. Fernandez. Sheriff Fernandez had a palatial summer place on Pickerel Pond, well known for its marvelous fishing; he often entertained dignitaries and friends from nearby Old Town. The living conditions for the soldiers, however, were far from what Mr. Fernandez knew. They bivouacked in tents for long durations and simulated battle conditions with frequent war exercises all while learning to use their heavy equipment proficiently. While there, the engineers built a bombing range in a bog south of the runway and constructed other needed air base installations, including gun emplacements. Bombers waiting for orders to travel the Great Circle Route to Europe often carried out bombing practice here, and other units from Dow Field used the Pickerel Pond area for training.[81]

Pickerel Pond airstrip today. It was built by the 924th Engineer Regiment in 1943. *Author's collection.*

The arrival of the engineers brought the population of Dow Field to 4,406. The population of the base changed daily, however, with the arrival and departure of 200 to 250 airplanes and crews monthly bound for Europe. The Air Transport Command used Dow Field to ferry bombers overseas while the base was still under the jurisdiction of the 1st Air Force. Before beginning their long flights, Dow Field personnel thoroughly briefed crews, medically cleared them, mechanically prepared the aircraft and supplied the airplanes with aviation fuel and the crews with whatever supplies they needed to make the journey. In Europe, enough airplanes were on hand to begin bombing Germany itself. The first such attack occurred on January 27, 1943, against Wilhelmshaven.[82] The *Memphis Belle* took part in subsequent bombings. The 8th Air Force paid dearly for these daylight precision-bombing attacks as unescorted bombers met fierce fighter resistance over the Reich. Closer to the target, murderous German flack sought to bring down the bombers. Those early crews, many of whom came through Bangor, suffered higher mortality rates than the island-hopping U.S. Marines in the South Pacific. In the months of May and June, 38 percent of crews were lost; subsequent months were not much better.[83] Still, General Henry H. Arnold, commanding general of the army air forces, promised that American factories would produce 115,000 new war planes that year for which crews were already in training. He also promised that Japan itself would come under wide-scale bombing in the near future. The pace of the war increased, driven by the production capacity of American industry.

One plane and crew that came through Dow Field that spring was destined to take part in the most daring and courageous air attack of the entire war—the August 1 low-level raid on the Nazi-held Romanian oil fields at Ploesti, dubbed by war planners as "Tidal Wave." After servicing by the major repair and line maintenance sections at Dow Field, a group made up entirely of civilian workers, the B-24 bomber named by its crew *Tondelao* took off from Dow Field on June 9, along with other bombers of the 389th Bombardment Group. They were at the air base for a few days preparing for their North Atlantic flight to Europe, where they joined other bomb groups as part of the 8th Air Force. Inside the *Tondelao* were ten men, the normal crew assigned to this bomber type; Staff Sergeant Ross L. Koch occupied one of the two waist gunner positions. A native of Grand Junction, Colorado, the soft-spoken airman of twenty-two had joined the army air forces prior to Pearl Harbor. Little did he know, as his aircraft left Bangor, that he was on an adventure of a lifetime, and that, to his knowledge, he would be the only wartime survivor of that original crew.

Tidal Wave was the collective brainchild of both President Roosevelt and British prime minister Winston Churchill. The genesis of the idea emerged from the Casablanca Conference as war leaders sought ways to strike decisive blows at Hitler's war machine. Air force leaders charged Colonel Jacob Smart, one of General Arnold's protégés, to develop an attack plan. Smart reasoned that a low-altitude attack of as little as fifty feet off the ground would completely surprise German defenses since they knew Americans liked to bomb normally from altitudes of twenty thousand to twenty-five thousand feet. German radar would also have a more difficult time detecting a low-run raid. If successful, a knockout of the Ploesti oil fields and refineries promised to shorten the war by six months since the facilities provided 60 percent of fuel and oil for the Nazi war machine; it was an alluring goal and worth any price.[84]

Smart assigned the attack to the 9th Air Force based in Benghazi, Libya, commanded by General Lewis H. Brereton. Brereton had only two heavy B-24 bombardment groups; he needed more to carry out this ambitious attack. Consequently, he borrowed three B-24 bombardment groups from the 8th Air Force, including the 389th. Planners preferred the B-24 bomber as it had a longer range and carried more bombs than the B-17. Sergeant Koch and his group landed in Benghazi by mid-July and immediately started training for the August 1 attack. Training consisted of low-level bombing practice of mock targets set up in the desert just outside Benghazi. The bomb groups needed to travel 2,300 miles round trip from Libya's coast northeast to the Balkan peninsula to inside Romania and then return; no nearer bases in Italy were yet available. Tidal Wave called for each bomb group to have a definite target; Koch's group had the cracking plant at Campina some 8 miles outside Ploesti itself.[85]

On Sunday, August 1, 177 heavily laden bombers took off seconds apart from the desert airfields. Koch's bomb group was the last to lift off; all five bomb groups were in the air by 5:00 a.m. In an October 2, 1944 story in the *Bangor Daily Commercial*, Koch described the scene over the Mediterranean Sea: "There were more B-24s in the sky then, than I'd ever seen in my life before. The sight was beautiful." Mishaps, though, beset this strategic raid from the very beginning. A bomber crashed and burned on takeoff; another suddenly fell from the sky into the Aegean Sea. Once over Bulgaria, the surging bombers ran into unexpected banks of cumulus clouds and lost visual contact among them. Planners forbade crews from using radios to reestablish contact because that would alert unsuspecting Germans. The biggest setback occurred when the lead group mistook a crucial IP, or initial point, and turned prematurely short of the target. By the time that group realized its mistake, corrected its course and turned toward Ploesti with a following bomb group in tow, the attackers had lost the element of surprise and gave German defenders time to reorient their 88s or anti-aircraft batteries for low-level defense. Although vastly more spread out now, the three other bomb groups proceeded as planned. All the Americans courageously pressed on.[86]

Koch and his 389th reached their target as scheduled. "We were flying very low and dropping our bombs at a two-hundred-foot altitude—then we would drop practically to the ground to minimize danger from anti-aircraft fire. There were about fifty-five enemy fighters attacking us—they would try to fly under our ships, and would occasionally hit the ground and be blown to bits." As a waist gunner on one side of *Tondelao*, Sergeant Koch was extremely busy with his .50-caliber machine gun warding off enemy attackers. Over the target, the 389th achieved success. "The target was completely in flame—and covered with smoke," recalled Koch. "I know where our bombs hit—right squarely across the gasoline cracking plant, which was our target. They caved one whole side of the building in—an important objective, because the cracking plant is where the crude oil is converted into gasoline. It was burning fiercely in a second. The flames leaped very high—after we left the target, we could see the light for at least a hundred miles."

Other bomb groups were less fortunate but dropped their bombs despite extreme confusion in the air from changed bombing runs and intense enemy opposition. Of the 163[87] planes that reached the Ploesti targets, 41 were lost in the fierce battle over the oil fields. Another 13 aircraft were lost in the effort. More than 530 airmen were killed, wounded or made prisoner. While this American attack failed to shorten the war as planned, it temporarily reduced German oil production by more than 40 percent for several months.[88] The attacks on Ploesti by American bombers of the 15th Air Force continued over the next year until the Russian army captured the fields. In total, the army air forces lost more than 270 bombers with 2,200 Americans killed.

Life in Bangor that middle war year took on the effect of humdrum non-normality. The government implemented a point rationing system for canned goods that further confused consumers and bemused shopkeepers. The city fretted over how to keep its roads in repair with the short supply of oil-based asphalt. The drafting of police and fire department personnel alarmed city officials. Employers complained about the lack of eligible workers. Colonel Valentine dispatched soldiers from Dow Field to help area farmers pick the ripening vegetable crops, an incongruous role for soldiers while their compatriots were being shot down in combat zones. Young

Later Romanian oil fields bombing by the 15th Air Force. *Lee Sirabella.*

military wives of soldiers based at Dow Field flooded the city looking for adequate housing; little was available. The rate of juvenile delinquency doubled from the previous year. The popular chairman of the city council and head of the city's civil defense program, Curtis M. Hutchins, resigned to take a commission in the navy. A special community church service at St. John's Episcopal Church in mid-March drew in community and military leaders. Worshipers filled the five-hundred-seat sanctuary, sang "Onward Christian Soldiers" and other patriotic hymns and offered prayers for peace, victory and protection for Bangor's military personnel. When Reverend John A. Furrer, rector of St. John's, read the names of the parish's sons and daughters now gone to fight, it reminded all gathered there about the current cost of this war. St. John's was only one of the city's many houses of worship that had seen its young people march off to unknown fates.

Air raid practices continued. Some Bangoreans remained confused about the signals, so officials put a new system into place that spring. The sounding of the city's fire and air raid sirens at an even pitch for three minutes was the first signal, dubbed "blue." This signal meant that enemy planes were approaching and that residents should extinguish all lights; streetlights were dimmed but remained lit. On the second signal, dubbed "red," the sirens wailed for three minutes denoting that enemy bombers were nearly overhead. All streetlights were turned off, and traffic stopped. Bangoreans were to seek shelter at home or in designated air raid shelters. The third signal in this battery, dubbed "white," signaled "all clear." Streetlights were turned back on, and local radio stations would broadcast an all-clear announcement over local radio stations. No sirens sounded. Still, compliance was less than perfect. Chief air raid warden Richard C. Pendleton, who succeeded Briggs the previous year when Briggs left for military service, retorted to an angry motorist who refused to follow this procedure, "You won't be so smart when the Japs get here."

The army's First Service Command conducted a surprise evening simulated air raid attack on July 21 to test Bangor's defenses. All air raid components went into play flawlessly as four B-25 bombers raced toward Bangor from the coast. The filter center alerted Dow Field, which was ready with its antiaircraft guns to shoot the bombers from the sky if they penetrated protective air space. As the bombers turned and headed south, the public's response pleased Bangor's civil defense officials. The filter center hummed with activity that evening. By late fall, though, civil defense officials had inactivated this component of civil defense because they determined then that the likelihood of an aerial attack on Bangor was extremely remote.

One bright spot in Bangor's life was its children's involvement in the war effort. Girl Scouts collected books as part of the Victory Book Drive. Organizers then gave these books to soldiers and inductees. Many books were donated to the library at Dow Field. Elementary schoolchildren actively participated in scrap drives; collected fat, packed boxes for needy children overseas; and sold war stamps and bonds. The Abraham Lincoln School sold enough bonds to purchase a PT-19 Fairchild pilot training plane. This plane carried a plaque on the side of its fuselage with the school's name. Other elementary schools in the city raised enough money to purchase jeeps, gliders, army trucks, hospital beds and ambulances. In a twist of fate, Elmer Blake from Bangor, an army ambulance driver in France, pulled a new Dodge ambulance from the motor pool and noticed that its cost had been raised by students at Garland Junior High School. The summer before, two young brothers, George and John Quirk, helped to organize a Junior Marine Corps. A local marine recruiter assisted the aspiring lads with drills; soon this group numbered forty Bangor boys. Proud of their accomplishment, the Quirk brothers wrote to the president and told him what they were up to. FDR responded through his

Bangor children, 1944. *Author's collection.*

secretary Grace Tully. In her letter, she congratulated the boys and conveyed the best wishes of the commander-in-chief. Governor Sewall also sent his congratulations. At the high school, the male youth participated in commando physical fitness training. Instructors set up an elaborate obstacle course behind the Harlow Street building and the adjoining public library. There, a number of challenging events helped to improve the youths' physical conditioning needed for future military service.

News that summer cheered Bangoreans. Mussolini resigned in late July; Italy agreed to surrender terms by early September.[89] FDR, like an athletic coach, called it "One Up and Two to Go." War-weary residents now saw some light at the end of the tunnel. The Germans, though, dug in and savagely resisted Allied advances up into the soft underbelly of Europe.

At Dow Field, the engineer battalions shipped out to combat zones. The first to leave in July was the 1913th Engineer Aviation Battalion. Their destination was the CBI, or China/Burma/India, theater. The 924th Headquarters and Service Section soon followed on its way to Europe. In

September, the 1905th left for India to work on the Ledo Road. Finally, the 1906th left the base toward the end of the year; its destination was also the CBI. The equipment for each engineer battalion filled approximately 115 freight cars that traveled on the base's spur to the Maine Central Railroad tracks at nearby Northern Maine Junction. From there, trains brought troops and equipment to different ports of embarkation.

At the Armistice Day observance, Colonel Valentine spoke to Bangoreans gathered at West Market Square about the importance of a strong national defense, in war and in peace, "to guard us against the aggression of the world." He also presented an Air Medal to the mother of airman Joseph M. Clark, who was presently a prisoner in a German POW camp, "for exceptionally meritorious achievement, while participating in five separate bomber combat missions over enemy occupied Continental Europe." Mrs. Ida M. Clark of Clinton Court in Bangor graciously accepted the medal and glanced at the new service flag just unfurled and draped across Main Street. On the large flag were two stars, one blue to represent the more than three thousand young Bangoreans fighting in the war and one gold to represent the thirteen who had already made the "supreme sacrifice." Many more followed.

Colonel Valentine's Armistice Day presentation was one of his last public appearances. The army air forces reassigned the popular base commander, who had been at Dow Field for almost fifteen months. His successor was Colonel Sigmund F. Landers from the army air base in Charleston, South Carolina. He soon faced the biggest challenge of any of his predecessors.

When Colonel Landers arrived at Dow, he found a reduced force at the base. Only 636 soldiers remained at the end of December after the departure of the last of the engineers and other troops due to reorganizations and reassignments. Base headquarters, the hospital detachment and an aviation squadron were all that remained. Then came the hard-to-understand directive from the War Department placing Dow Field on a standby status and changing its jurisdiction from 1st Air Force to Air Service Command. In a January 4, 1944 memorandum to Colonel Landers, headquarters of the Air Service Command referred to Dow Field as being in "inoperative status" and that remaining personnel should be put to work doing guard duty until the army corps of engineers assumed control of the base for housekeeping; the senior engineer officer then would assume command of Dow Field. The only exception to this Air Service Command directive was a unique P-39 project. The Operations Maintenance Department of the sub-depot was in the midst of the reassembly of a dozen war-weary P-39 fighter aircraft. Each of these planes had flown a minimum of four hundred hours and essentially

P-39 testing program with First Lieutenant Sidney Dyke. *John Miller—Vintage Wings.*

needed to be rebuilt. First Lieutenant Sidney A. Dyke headed up a small temporary flight test section and air tested each refurbished fighter for ten hours, taking it through various maneuvers. Once passed, a ferry pilot flew the aircraft to Las Vegas, Nevada. From there, another ferry pilot flew the P-39 to Alaska, where a Russian pilot picked it up and took it over the Bering Strait into Siberia; this project was part of Lend-Lease.[90]

Standby status in effect meant that the base was shut down. The civilian workers at the air base worried about their jobs; military personnel reasoned that a useful role for the base could be found. After all, the base was only four years old and by this time represented $10 million of taxpayers' money. And the world was still at war. Senator Brewster tried to explain this move in light of the anticipated eventual victory over Nazi Germany "as a preview of what must be expected in increasing measure as the war moves on." "Washington," he explained, "is looking forward to the liquidation of its manifold interests and activities [military bases]." Colonel Landers, though, went to work and advocated with his superiors by letter and by phone to keep the base open. He worked vigorously to keep up morale. On February 17, 1944, he achieved success when he received word from the Air Transport Command in Washington that Dow Field was reinstated as a port of aerial embarkation under the jurisdiction of the Air Transport Command.[91]

With this positive change in status, the air base took on a whole new life as Station #3, North Atlantic Wing of the Air Transport Command. Dow Field joined sister stations at Presque Isle and Grenier Field in Manchester, New Hampshire, as staging areas for thousands of aircrews leaving for battle in Europe. The Allies needed these new bomber crews as they prepared to invade the European continent from across the English Channel and to sustain the stepped-up bombing campaign of Nazi Germany. Fighting in Italy was bogged down with stiff Germany resistance, and a new Allied initiative was needed. War planners hoped to bring the war with Germany to an end that year. The big push was on.[92]

Newly arrived soldiers quickly helped base personnel organize a "processing center" at Dow Field. The purpose of the processing center was to efficiently expedite the movement of aircrews to the European Theater of Operations (ETO) by speeding them on their way over the Great Circle Route. Personnel constructed covered hallways that connected together several warehouse buildings formerly used by the quartermaster corps. This center, resembling an assembly line, was ready by April 1. When an aircrew arrived, the airmen reported first to a "control center." Here, they turned over their hand-carried records for processing and updating. The crew then split up, the officers reporting to an "engineering" section while the enlisted men went off to the Red Cross counter, where volunteers served them coffee and doughnuts. Engineering asked the officers, meanwhile, a number of questions about their aircraft. Any reported problems were referred to other departments on the base for remediation to ensure that the departing aircraft was in first-class condition. The crew then came back together and, joining other aircrews, entered the orientation section. There, Dow Field personnel reviewed a variety of information, including what crew members might expect when they arrived at the ETO. After orientation, the crew moved through an emergency equipment section, where they had the opportunity to look at different lifesaving devices preparatory to the long flight across the Atlantic. Then the crew passed through a medical clearance section. Here, the base surgeon and other medical staff conducted a final medical and dental check of each crew member. Next was a stop in a personal affairs section, where processing center personnel quizzed airmen about any changes they might desire to make to insurance, allotments and

Processing center—engineering section. (Notice the Dow Field runway schema on the back wall.) *Bangor Public Library.*

Last medical clearance. (Notice the crew bailout posters for B-17 and B-24 on the back wall.) *Bangor Public Library.*

Officers' billeting desk, processing center. *Bangor Public Library.*

Bombers waiting to go. (Notice the B-24 in the foreground being fueled and a B-24 landing on the far right.) *Bangor Public Library.*

other financially related matters. A stop in a personnel section brought the crew up to date about payrolls, pay vouchers and other money issues. At the stop in the base finance section, crew members had a chance to purchase war bonds. The exhausted crew finally moved to billeting, the last section of the processing center. Here, base personnel assigned the crew to quarters until base operations cleared their aircraft for departure.[93]

Dow Field personnel were kept busy with the arrival and departure of combat crews. Mess hall personnel prepared meals and lunches for departing crews. Base soldiers carried on all the housekeeping necessary for the transient airmen. As the spring wore on, an increasing number of crew arrived. In May, over 340 aircraft left for overseas destinations. This number increased in June to almost 500. Crews landing at Dow Field came from as far away as Lincoln and Kearney AAF air bases, both in Nebraska.[94] At times, as many as 140 B-17 and B-24 bombers, each with a ten-man crew, lined the runways waiting for departure.[95] And the sixth of that month was a special day, long awaited by the free world; the Allies launched Operation Overlord, or D-Day, when they attacked the fortified coast of Normandy, France. Bangoreans flocked to houses of worship, which opened their doors for prayer and meditation that Tuesday. Dow soldiers and Bangor citizens knew that the big push was on.

10

FROM THE WAR FRONTS

"I wish you could be assured of the comparative safety of Oxford, come what may. Unlike Cambridge, Oxford is not a military objective…German bombers will at least choose easily available places," wrote young Bangorean Robert G. Cumming to his parents, Dr. and Mrs. Charles Cumming of Hammond Street, in a February 1940 letter. The war in Europe was on, and for Robert, a Rhodes scholar, his continued study there was of growing concern for his family. As the fighting intensified that spring, the State Department issued warnings to Americans in Europe and advised them to leave. Robert, along with 719 other Americans, boarded the *President Roosevelt*, an American liner, in early June at Galway, Ireland, and left for New York. The *Manhattan*, another American ship, left Genoa, Italy, about this same time with almost 2,000 Americans aboard, who were fleeing the fighting in Europe. Washington notified the warring nations about the passage of these ships so that they did not become targets of enemy submarines as the ships sailed through war zones. Cumming reached New York safely, much to the relief of his parents. Dunkirk was over; the Battle of Britain was about to begin.[96]

Union Street's C. Leo Smith found working at the Sears Roebuck store on Harlow Street a little mundane; he wanted to do some traveling and signed up for the merchant marine. Then the war broke out. Now he served as a crew member on a large oil tanker traversing the Caribbean Sea destined for an East Coast port. It was early Sunday afternoon, April 12, 1942, when a torpedo from a submarine slammed into the zigzagging tanker. "The force of the explosion shook the ship like a dog shaking a rat and hurled a column of water two hundred feet over the hull. I was…hurled to my knees by the impact and drenched with brine and oil," the twenty-nine-year-old Smith later recalled. As the crew clambered into lifeboats and pulled away from the doomed vessel, the culprit submarine surfaced and began to fire shells from its two deck guns once the tanker's crew was clear of the hulk. Finally, the ship caught fire until it was a raging inferno. Leaking oil burned and set the sea ablaze for three miles around the dying ship. The submarine's captain sailed his craft close to the lifeboats and asked if anyone needed medical attention or if food was needed. And in a final act of chivalry, the captain gave the lifeboat occupants bearings to the closest land and left with the parting words, "Don't take it too hard, this is war you know." The tanker's crew identified the submarine as Italian, allies of Nazi Germany. Enemy submarines ravaged American shipping just off the Atlantic coast that spring.[97] The U.S. Navy rescued Smith and his shipmates the next day.

Stanley Novak's twenty-seventh birthday was far different from any he celebrated growing up in his home on Pine Street. He was now an engineer on a B-17 as it climbed into formation over the English countryside on a spring day in 1943. Without warning, he found himself tumbling in space toward earth. "I must have blacked out from the explosion as the plane flew to pieces," he remembered. Unfrightened, Stanley watched with a trancelike fascination as the earth grew larger. Instinctively, he reached for the parachute's shoulder straps; he did not remember if he were wearing one. He felt the straps and pulled the ripcord handle, but nothing happened. Still undisturbed, he then flung his right arm across his body, causing the steel handle of the ripcord to hit his left shoulder strap. The parachute deployed with a snap and filled with lifesaving cushioning air; Novak was only one thousand feet over an English field. An English farmer rescued him; he spent several months in military hospitals due to injuries. Midair collisions of bombers maneuvering into position through often-murky English skies took the lives of hundreds of Allied airmen. Novak barely escaped this fate.

"It's remarkable what you can do when you have to," was how Bangor's Arlene Hibbard described her days as an army nurse in an evacuation hospital in France just after the D-Day landings. There, she helped treat the horribly wounded young men with torn limbs and gaping holes in their bodies. Some suffered from combat fatigue as they staggered about as if drunk. Nurse Hibbard and others of the medical staff also ministered to captured injured German soldiers while off in the distance they heard the army's guns that fired at German aircraft. She credited the saving of countless lives to whole blood and plasma: "I get awfully tired…but it's a thankful tiredness. We know we are needed, and appreciated."

"A lightning thing" was how Bette Barker of Bangor described her meeting Donald Kilpatrick Jr. Both were seniors at the University of Maine and both were student leaders when they met at a meeting on campus only months before Pearl Harbor. "We clicked right away," and click they did. On December 7, 1942, they were married and lived lives shaped by war. Donald, an outstanding college athlete, scholar and leader, trained to be a pilot; he earned his wings in October 1943. Bette was with him whenever possible but returned to Bangor that fall to have their baby. Their daughter, Nancy, was born in January 1944, and for an all too short time, the young family was together as Donald went through his final training as a bomber pilot at Westover Field; he received orders in early May to fly overseas. Bette and Nancy returned to Bangor to stay with Bette's mother, Natalie Barker. At the beginning of his flight to Europe, he landed his Liberator bomber at Dow Field for the first night's stay. He surprised Bette when he showed up at 116 Webster Avenue that evening in a borrowed Jeep from the Dow motor pool. Early the next morning, Donald bade his wife and child a teary but optimistic goodbye. The young lovers' parting embrace on the doorstep was evanescent but passionate; war called. Donald jumped into the Jeep and quickly drove up Hammond Street the half mile to Dow Field. Soon thereafter, he left for Europe. The young couple never saw each other again. Once in England, the 8th Air Force assigned Donald, crew and craft to the 492nd Bomb Group, dubbed by Doolittle as "the Hard Luck Group." German fighters shot Donald's B-24 from the sky over Bernburg on July 7; it was their fifteenth and last bombing mission. Two years passed before Bette knew what happened to Donald, initially listed as "missing in action." On that fateful day, Donald and others of the crew escaped the bomber as it spiraled earthward. German soldiers on the ground, though, shot at the parachuting airmen; a bullet killed Donald before he touched the earth. He was but twenty-two.[98]

"The shell hit a tree and burst into hundreds of fragments. Two of us were hit, and a third man was killed instantly," was how Clayton Gould of Otis Street in Bangor remembered his miracle. It was the Battle of the Bulge launched just before Christmas 1944 by the German army as Hitler's last great western offensive to push the advancing Allied armies back. Gould and his buddies were part of an anti-tank team; it was dark, snowing and cold when their officers ordered them to advance. The Germans responded with a barrage of eighty-eight-millimeter mortar shells. Eight pieces of one of

The Kilpatricks: Bette, holding Nancy, and Donald, 1944. *Author's collection.*

these shells wounded Clayton, but the one piece that could have ended his life then and there instead hit the metal cover of his missal that he carried with him in his shirt pocket over his heart. The shell fragment caused a dent; the missal made a miracle.

Early in the war, Robert King, nineteen, gave his fellow Bangoreans some ideas about the Japanese as fighters. The Savage Street resident visited his father after seventeen months' service in the U.S. Marine Corps, three months of which he spent fighting on Guadalcanal. "Don't make any mistake about it, the Japanese are good fighters. They are suicidal." Americans came to realize this as reports filtered back from the fighting fronts. The Japanese are "not to be trusted and are tricky in battle…The boys found out early that the cries of some Japanese for water was only an invitation to move within range of a hand grenade." The fighting characteristics of the Japanese warrior and his preference to die over surrender increasingly governed American war policy in the Pacific Theater of Operations.

Bangor native Donald Libby was wounded thirteen times as he stormed the beaches of Tarawa with his fellow marines. In one of the bloodiest battles of the Pacific islands, Libby actually never made it onto shore. Shrapnel from an enemy mortar shell exploded ammunition in his landing craft that in turn struck him in the right leg. When he tried to leap from his landing craft, machine gun bullets coming from on shore tore into his right foot, removed a toe and further injured his right leg. Then, as he limped ashore, a bullet from a Japanese rifle struck him, followed by another bullet that hit him in his back near his right lung. His landing craft then exploded, and its bursting debris shattered his left leg above the ankle. Moments later, Japanese machine gun bullets thudded into his left leg. He continued to stagger ashore, now with thirteen holes in his body, until he reached the side of a beached American landing craft. There, he clung to a cable from its side for hours as he weakened from his wounds. It grew dark. Suddenly, he heard sloshing around the back of the beached landing craft. A voice inquired if he were a marine. Libby responded that he was. Then the inquirer asked him where he was from. Maine, responded Libby. Suddenly, this individual lunged at Libby with a swinging bayonet; it was a Japanese marine. Libby dodged while being nicked in the left hand by the wheeling blade. The Japanese marine lunged again and nicked Libby's right hand. The third lunge by the Japanese was his last. He lost his balance. This gave Libby, adrenaline pumping, the chance to grab the bayonet from the Japanese man. Libby recalled little of what occurred next other than, "I guess I just went crazy." The Japanese marine lay dead; Americans rescued Libby shortly thereafter. Prior to his enlistment in the marines, Libby had worked at Dow Field in the Post Exchange.

It seemed like "forever" as Adrian Chisholm fell through the air into the Pacific Ocean fifty yards from his ship, the USS *Princeton*, an aircraft carrier involved in fall 1944 sea battles with the Japanese in the Philippine Sea. A bomb from an attacking Japanese fighter set off a series of explosions, one of which catapulted Chisholm into the ocean and eventually doomed his ship. He landed amid others, found floating debris and was rescued two hours later by sailors manning a whale boat. Chisholm's watch stopped at 10:06 a.m., the time the marine hit the water. Now, he was glad to be back at his Essex Street home.

"I was taken off the crew a few days before the ill-fated mission,"[99] wrote William Bunga to Edgar Keith of Bangor. Bunga had trained for six months as the copilot on Austin Keith's crew of eleven men that was needed to man the B-29 Superfortress bomber. Austin, Edgar's only son, was the airplane commander, or pilot, of the massive aircraft designed specifically to bomb the Japanese homeland. After three bombing missions, the army air forces removed Bunga; this twist of fate saved Bunga. On the fourth bombing mission, Austin's bomber and another B-29 collided. Both crews plummeted into the depths of the Pacific Ocean. No one survived. Bunga went on to complete thirty-four bombing missions and survived the war.[100]

11

ONE DOWN, ONE TO GO

For the time being, the light rain stopped and the clouds scattered as the B-17G 43-3803[101] lifted off the runway of Kearney Army Air Base, Nebraska, at 6:20 a.m., headed for Dow Field. The ten young men aboard looked forward to their day's journey across the United States that Tuesday, July 11, 1944; they were scheduled to arrive in Bangor at 12:30 p.m. From there, after processing and like so many hundreds of crews before them, they would ferry the bomber across the Atlantic to England. They had trained for many months. Now, they were going to war. Second Lieutenant John T. Cast, twenty-seven, piloted the craft; Second Lieutenant John W. Drake, twenty-one, sat in the copilot's seat. Second Lieutenant William F. Hudgens, twenty-one, navigated the aircraft. The other officer on board, Second Lieutenant Robert S. Talley, twenty-six, did not have much to do that day, as he was the bombardier. Some of the enlisted men, though, were busier than Talley. Engineer Wayne B. McGravan, twenty-four, helped the pilot and copilot with engine adjustments and fuel usage, and Cecil L. Murphy, twenty-one, radioed the aircraft's position at various checkpoints as it flew eastward. Gunners James A. Benson, twenty-one; Gerald V. Biddle, twenty-three; John H. Jones, twenty; and Clarence M. Waln, twenty-two—all sergeants except Jones, who was a corporal—enjoyed the view. The bomber flew over Moline, Illinois; Toledo, Ohio; and then Syracuse, New York, where it made radio contact at 10:10 a.m. The flight proceeded on schedule. At 10:55 a.m., Cecil Murphy contacted Grenier Field in Manchester, New Hampshire.

The planned route in Maine called for a flight path over Auburn, then Augusta and finally into Bangor.[102]

Cast and Drake grew worried as they peered ahead. Large, ominous, dark thunderclouds loomed. Together, they guided the B-17 northeastward some sixty miles off the prescribed course with the idea of flying around the thunderclouds. Still, the change in course was not enough, and soon the craft was pummeled by hail, sheets of rain and lightning strikes. This same storm caused considerable damage to the countryside below.[103] The storm knocked out their radio, they lost their bearings and they were over strange mountainous country shrouded by low-hanging clouds. Cast brought the craft down to better see landmarks below while Hudgens desperately scanned his maps. Soon, the B-17 was over Rangely Lake, a lake surrounded by high mountains; it was about 11:30 a.m. For the next hour and a half, Cast circled the lake at times so low that curious residents could see the aircraft's rivets.[104] Fuel ran low, and Cast needed to bring the craft safely down to save his crew. A small emergency airstrip lay to the northwest of the town of Rangely, but the ceiling was only 1,000 feet; no one on the crew saw it. Cast decided to bring the B-17 down on Mooselookmeguntic Lake, a nearby lake to Rangely and one the B-17 had also circled. This lake was longer and more suitable to a water crash landing. He climbed to the northwest intending to do a dogleg down into Mooselookmeguntic.[105] As he banked in the mist and fog, Cast saw 3,500-foot Deer Mountain rise in front of him. Despite heroic efforts and a seventy-degree bank to port, his left wing caught the upper half of large trees. This impact caused the bomber to cartwheel into the forest below. The crashing aircraft gouged an opening through the forest canopy for a length of 800 feet and from a width of a few feet to 260 feet. Three of the four whirling, straining Wright motors flew hundreds of feet into the woods from the crash site. Craft and crew were rent asunder. "Everything was just like a giant lawn mower went through there,"[106] recalled Lee Sirabella, who was with the signal corps at Dow Field and responsible for taking the accident photographs. Back at Dow, operations headquarters began a search. Two days later, Major Lamont of that section spotted the wreckage.[107] For ten young American airmen, their war ended on a Maine mountainside.

At Dow Field that summer, the pace of war activity accelerated as a port of embarkation for aircraft and combat crews leaving for Europe. The processing center handled over seven hundred crews and aircraft in July, nearly double the number it had processed in June. Already, the army air forces gained mastery of the skies over Nazi-held territory. Rickenbacker, the summer before, had indicated that Germany must be broken "from the

Pre-flight briefing. (Notice all the instructions on the blackboard.) *Bangor Public Library.*

Opposite, top: An aircrew practices using a life raft, 1944. *Bangor Historical Society.*

Opposite, bottom: At the ready for air sea rescue, the 921st Company Boat (Aviation) stationed at Bar Harbor. *Bangor Public Library.*

inside" through massive bombing. (For the Japanese, he was less sanguine; they did not surrender. Still, he predicted a miracle that "will shock the world.")[108] Processing center personnel prepared crews for their Atlantic crossing. For officers, the preflight briefing was crucial. Here army weathermen and other specialists disseminated information to ensure a successful flight as they hopped their way over to Europe. Two-engine airplanes first stopped at Goose Bay, Labrador, while four-engine bombers flew on to Gander, Newfoundland, as their first stop.[109] Crews practiced for this perilous journey over the ocean. A unique service of the army air forces stood by if an air sea rescue of a downed crew was necessary. The 921st Company Boat (Aviation) was stationed at Bar Harbor for this purpose.[110]

The Air Transport Command named Dow Field as a staging area in early June. A special classification team arrived to direct the screening and interviewing of 2,400 enlisted men prior to their assignment to air bases

1379 BU - 3 OCT,44 - G-502.38 - TRAINING UNIT
(1)

G-501.92
(11)

worldwide.[111] Base personnel, in addition to preparing departing bomber crews, now were also kept busy with these enlisted men from other parts of the army air forces. Colonel James C. Jensen, who succeeded Colonel Landers as base commander on June 9, found Dow Field a beehive of activity.[112] Fourteen mess halls were up and running by July to provide the meals for aircrews and soldiers. Six bakers and twenty-three cooks staffed each kitchen. But Colonel Jensen had more than food to concern himself with when he first arrived; he had to deal with a growing venereal disease rate among soldiers. The base surgeon expressed his concern to the point that the base commander restricted certain areas of Bangor as off-limits to base soldiers. Jensen issued a stiff order to all personnel at Dow Field that generally identified the lower area of French, York, Hancock and Boyd Streets for their high VD rate and for possible houses of prostitution.[113] Embarrassed city officials worked with the new base commander on the problem. "The problem of social disease has been one that has given our Health Department more concern this year than for any of the previous years. The condition has been aggravated by the fact that the concentration of men here has caused an influx of undesirables," wrote city manager Horace Estey in his 1944 annual report.

War news that summer continued to improve. The marines and army recaptured Guam from the Japanese after a three-week battle. In Europe, American and Allied forces marched into Paris in late August.[114] At Dow Field, aircrews continued to leave for Europe. It was not unusual for as many as fifty planes to be lined up on the runways in the morning waiting for takeoff. The noise of the revving motors and whirling propellers of B-17s, B-24s, B-25s and A-26s shook the base and surrounding city.[115] Occasionally, a crash occurred at takeoff. On September 17, an A-26 two-man medium bomber on its way to Goose Bay, Labrador, lost power and crashed in Bangor's Church Street area; both crewmen were killed. Earlier, a four-engine bomber had crashed on takeoff on June 3, 1943, but all ten crew members survived. The safety record at the base was high, and crews carefully prepared for departure.

Dow Field hosted a Civil Air Patrol (CAP) cadet-training program in early August 1944. Eighty-five sixteen- to seventeen-year-old boys from all over Maine arrived at Union Station ready for a weeklong encampment. All were members of CAP cadet squadrons back home. And just like the soldiers when they arrived in Bangor, army trucks from the air base met them and brought them out to Hammond Street. Once on base, CAP officers assigned them to barracks. The cadets spent six hours each day in classroom instruction on

A B-24 crew ready to leave on the Great Circle Route. (Notice some crew members have on their May West life jacket and parachute.) *Bangor Public Library.*

topics ranging from military courtesy to chemical warfare. For two hours per day, the young cadets engaged in drill; cadets spent an additional hour in physical training. Dow officials gave the cadets a complete tour of the field's extensive flight line and an up-close look at a B-17 Flying Fortress. Cadets also examined the base's Link Trainer. The week ended with a retreat, or parade. This program helped prepare youth for enlistment in the army air forces; it was an effective recruitment tool. The U.S. Office of Civil Defense founded the Civil Air Patrol just prior to Pearl Harbor to mobilize volunteer civilian airmen and their equipment. In Maine, CAP carried out wartime duties such as conducting anti-submarine patrols off the coast and assisting the army in search and rescue operations.

Dow Field marked the thirty-seventh birthday of the army air forces on August 1 with an open house, one of several held during wartime. More than 3,000 Bangoreans attended the afternoon-long event. While the hangar line where workers prepared aircraft for departure and some other areas were off-limits, visitors toured the gymnasium, the chapel, the various officers' and enlisted men's clubs and WAC Hill. Soldiers representing different departments explained their work, and displays included the twelve-cylinder motors that powered the B-24 Liberator bomber. The Dow Field Band gave a 3:00 p.m. concert, and a retreat parade ceremony hosted by Colonel Jensen followed at 4:00 p.m. The growth of the army air forces from a three-man component of the signal corps in 1907 to more than 2.3 million men and women impressed Bangoreans, and they were a part of this history.

War news from both fronts continued to encourage Americans. Russian forces pressed their advance westward while Allied forces pressed their attack eastward, both aimed at the German heartland. In Japan, Tojo, the war premier, fell from power.[116] For the United States, then a country of 130 million people, the war costs mounted. The federal government spent an estimated $140 million a day by fall 1944 ($1.9 billion in today's dollars); American involvement in World War II totaled $200 billion to date ($2.7 trillion in today's dollars). The government sponsored frequent war loan drives to raise necessary cash, and this summer, Bangoreans experienced the fifth such fundraising effort. In this particular drive, the Bangor district was off to a slow start to meet its quota. At Dow Field, the opposite was true as Colonel Jensen implored his soldiers and civilian workers to support this latest bond drive. Colonel Jensen put the country's monetary needs in terms his people understood: "When the soldier is ready for combat, he must be equipped with certain basic weapons, such as a .30-caliber semi-automatic M1 Garand rifle (cost $35), a bayonet (cost $3.20) and at least four hand grenades (cost $2.40)." He also put these costs in AAF terms: "Bombs weighing up to 4,000 pounds cost up to $778. Another detail such as oxygen masks for the crew of a Flying Fortress cost about $40. To each mask is attached a regulator costing $60, and a $25 oxygen cylinder from which the flyer draws his breath of life." Colonel Jensen's approach proved successful as military and civilian personnel at the base exceeded preset quotas by 136 percent. Colonel Jensen also took an active part in the city's Community and War Chest Campaign that summer. The Bangor-Brewer Community Chest, Inc., headed by leading businessman Charles F. Bragg Jr., raised funds to support local eleemosynary agencies, one being the USO.

By mid-September, the positive war news from Europe prompted many Americans to think that Nazi Germany's surrender was imminent. In Bangor, the chamber of commerce released plans for a victory celebration. The chamber published its plan and encouraged citizens to cut out the schedule and keep it handy. Specifically, the victory celebration would begin with the ringing of all of the city's church bells for five minutes. Then, thirty minutes later, Bangoreans were to go to designated houses of worship for services.

A Victory Parade and rally would follow, its time to be determined by when the government announced the German surrender. The final listed activity was a street dance in West Market Square. These well-thought-out plans, unfortunately, were at best too optimistic; German resistance heightened as the Allied armies approached the Rhine; much hard fighting remained.

The Air Transport Command (ATC) base in Bangor continued its day-to-day war-winning work that fall. Headquarters transferred a fleet of thirteen C-46 transport planes from its base in Presque Isle to Bangor.[117] Over the next several months, these aircraft shipped cargo and personnel to all the bases in the North Atlantic Division. The ATC took on the guise of a great airline, shuttling supplies to its bases along the Great Circle Route and carrying mail to Europe. The army air forces, through its ATC, learned how to deal with arctic flight conditions. Harsh weather conditions no longer impeded the flow of men and materiel to the war zones in Europe. In a December open house at Dow Field, Bangoreans viewed how the ATC learned to deal with the harsh weather of the world's Arctic region. They watched the men of Squadron E parade by in white parkas carrying skis as part of an arctic rescue patrol. African Americans made up Squadron E and throughout the

A B-17 crew cleans snow off its bomber. (Notice the hangar in the background. It is still in use today.) *Bangor Public Library.*

The *Hag of Harderwyk* B-17 bomber and Dow Field civilian mechanics. *Bangor Public Library.*

war provided the guard duty functions at the base. Although Maine's winter weather taxed flight preparations, it did not slow the mission of cargo craft and bombers needed to press the attack on the Nazi homeland.

The lean, long body of the B-17 bomber now bore countless bullet holes and flak patches. Before, when the *Hag of Harderwyk* sat in the major repair hangar, it was on its way to Europe. Civilian workers that April 1943 worked on the oxygen system, the number two engine, the tail wheel and the all-important ball machine gun turret that hung below its belly. The B-17 required almost 150 man-hours of work of preparation before the *Hag* lifted off for Europe. Now safely back at Dow Field eighteen months later, the same civilian workers saw the battle damage; they also counted twenty-eight bombs painted on its fuselage, each bomb indicating a bombing mission—a testimony to its work over Nazi territory. And three dreaded swastikas, symbols of Hitler's Third Reich, marked the destruction of three Luftwaffe attackers.

The successful mission of bombers from Dow Field depended on the contribution of Bangoreans. Throughout the war, citizens worked closely with soldiers toward victory. Bangor's Junior Welfare League was but one of many civic organizations that made a difference in the daily life of the base. Volunteer members donated four hours each afternoon and four hours two evenings a week in the base library. Their work there helped to meet the "off-duty" needs of the field's soldiers. Other Bangor groups also sought to minister to the soldiers. Beth Israel Synagogue gave a Torah to Harold H. Gordon, the Jewish chaplain to the North American Division of the ATC, who served from Dow Field. Rabbi Gordon carried the sacred scroll, central to Jewish religious services, from base to base along the Great Circle Route as he ministered to the spiritual needs of Jewish airmen. Beth Israel's gift became known as the "Flying Torah" and traveled thousands of miles from Bangor bringing "comfort and courage" to soldiers during wartime.

"This war will be won by unrelenting labor of those of us who are still here," exhorted Lieutenant Colonel Olie Schurter, Dow's executive officer, at a sixth war loan drive rally in early December. Schurter described working conditions at some of the ATC's arctic bases to his audience. There, at these remote installations and landing fields, temperatures dropped to seventy-eight degrees below zero, snow depths reached 148 inches and winds whipped snow into mountainous drifts. Lee Sirabella, stationed during the

Bangor Junior Welfare League in the base library, 1945. *Bangor Public Library.*

Rabbi Harold Gordon with the Flying Torah. *Bangor Public Library.*

war at Narsarssuak or Bluie West I, the ATC base on the western reaches of Greenland, recalled "having to crawl across the [metal] runway on my hands and knees because it was too icy to walk across it…going downhill toward the fjord." Army engineers, early in the war, quickly constructed this Marsden Metal Matting runway for use by bombers on their way to Europe.[118] Still, according to Schurter, these harsh working conditions were nothing compared to what the frontline fighter in Europe experienced, where "biting cold and chill…never leaves the soldier in the…foxhole" or nothing compared to "the enervating, disease-breeding heat that the soldier in the South Pacific island[s] must face." At this same rally, base commander Jensen gave out monetary awards to civilian workers who suggested time and labor improvements to their work. Jensen passionately praised them and urged others to follow suit: "Every ounce of energy that you throw into your job; every spark of enthusiasm that you kindle in someone else's heart to work harder; every bit of added push that you give the job to be done—will make the war end that much sooner. And that is the thing all of us want most." Many of these workers used their cash winnings to purchase war bonds.

Bangor firefighters purchase war bonds, 1944. *Bangor Public Library.*

Americans strained to bring the war on both fronts to a speedy close. Late that November, massive B-29s began bombing raids of the Japanese homeland from bases in the Marianas, which were closer to Japan than the bases in India previously used. In Europe, where the Allied advances had achieved great momentum, American and British bombers continued to pound the German heartland. Still, just six days after Colonel Jensen spoke to his people at Dow Field about bringing the war to a speedy end, Hitler shocked the world with an offensive through the Ardennes Forests of Belgium and Luxembourg. The Battle of the Bulge, as it became known, cost thousands of American casualties and cast doubt on Nazi Germany's speedy demise.[119]

Snow swirled over the sleepy city and air base on Christmas morning. A large aircraft circled over the air base for the longest time, the drone of its four engines reverberating through the stillness. With visibility near zero, Captain Jim Crowley put the C-54 Skymaster down on a Dow runway. Because of weather, the ATC diverted its aircraft, destined for LaGuardia Field, to Bangor. The huge ship carried newly wounded from Europe's fighting. Base

Wounded arriving at Dow Field in specially equipped ATC C-54 Skymasters. *Bangor Public Library.*

Surgeon Lieutenant Colonel Morris and his staff met the airplane on the runway's edge and transported its patients to the base hospital. This was the beginning of many "evacuation flights" of America's war wounded into Dow Field, designated by the ATC as a debarkation hospital. Special equipment gingerly transported wounded soldiers from craft to care in the hospital's wards until they could be sent for long-term treatment in military hospitals across the United States. For Bangoreans, reading about these lifesaving flights brought the war's reality into their living rooms; the war with Hitler's Nazi Germany was a hard fight to the finish. One patient, Lieutenant John Bynum of Texas, described the German defenders as "those guys you just have to kill to get."

Allied forces reached the Rhine River, Germany's western frontier, on February 14 and crossed it three weeks later after prolonged fighting. The Russian army crossed Poland and pushed into East Prussia. In the Pacific, General MacArthur returned, landing in Luzon, the Philippines. The nearly month-long struggle to capture Iwo Jima cost more than twenty thousand American casualties; Americans worried about its human costs to conquer Japan.[120] Bangor's casualties mounted, with soldiers' obituaries now commonplace in the local papers.

War activity consumed Dow Field and reflected the country's effort to bring the European war to a successful finish. Warplanes arrived daily. The last built B-24 bomber, a stalwart weapon of the army air forces, passed through Dow on its way to Europe. The AAF reassigned many of its airmen to the ground forces to include men from Dow Field. They left in early February 1945. Colonel Jensen left for a new assignment later in the month. Jensen was much respected by Bangoreans. City manager Estey said of Jensen's departure: "This city has always been fortunate in that the local military base has been under the command of able leaders who appreciated the problems of the municipal officials. Colonel Jensen…was no exception to the rule, and his helpful cooperation should be a matter of public record."[121] Lieutenant Colonel Orie Schurter took over as base commander.

By spring 1945, Bangoreans, like most Americans, were inured to the hardships of war. They followed the news of the war intensely, hoping for word of its end. Still, the Germans held on despite the deadly firebombing of Dresden, a beautiful Renaissance city with little military value. British and American bombers pounded other German cities with more than forty thousand sorties in late March.[122] Hitler exhorted his troops, now made up of old men and young boys, to fight to the death; they didn't. German resistance began to crumble. In the Pacific, the 20th Air Force instituted low-level firebombing of Japanese cities with hundreds of B-29 bombers stationed in the Marianas. This apogee of American air power in the Far East spelled doom for the Japanese.

"Too bad he couldn't have lived to see the end of the war," said one resident, expressing the sentiment of Bangoreans when news of President Roosevelt's sudden death reached the Penobscot city. The news was so shocking that on Thursday afternoon, April 12, few knew what to do or say. City manager Estey and chairman of the city council George Peabody issued a proclamation calling on the citizens to pause in respect for America's fallen war leader. At Dow Field, all personnel stood at silent attention for one minute the next morning. Little else occurred, as a war still flamed.

News that Bangoreans and Americans hungered for came on May 8 when President Truman announced that Nazi Germany had unconditionally surrendered to Allied Forces the day before. The president declared that day to be V-E Day, or Victory in Europe Day. In Bangor, though, celebration was subdued in marked contrast to plans for a "thought but premature German surrender" the previous September. The most active places within the city

V-E service and memorial at Dow Field for President Roosevelt in front of base headquarters. (The headquarters building now faces Maine Avenue.) *Bangor Public Library.*

were houses of worship open for religious thanksgiving services. Citizens and soldiers knew that America was still at war in the Pacific—a war that promised to go into 1946. War Department reports showed 750,000 American war casualties in Europe; no one could predict the number of casualties in Japan.

War-weary and battered bombers began to make their way home from Europe through Dow Field by the end of May. The first large group of twenty bombers packed with 400 returning airmen landed on Friday, May 25, refueled after an 1,800-mile flight from Greenland and left for Bradley Field in Connecticut. Only days later, seventy-two bombers with 1,600 8th Air Force veterans aboard landed. The men stayed overnight, swamped the Post Exchange, swapped war stories and departed for Bradley the next day. The joyous crews, happy to be home in America, scooped up Bangor soil, posed for pictures and drank fresh milk, an unknown amenity in Europe. At Bradley, crews received brief furloughs and then were reassigned for Pacific war duty. For them, it was one down, one to go.

U.S. Maine senator Ralph O. Brewster with the crew of a B-24 bomber, 44th Bombardment Group at Dow Field, June 1945. To Senator Brewster's left is Lieutenant Colonel Orie Schurter. *Bangor Historical Society.*

The parade of bombers through the ATC base went on for more than a month. By the end of June, nearly six thousand airmen and their aircraft had flown through Bangor. Some of the planes already had war renown. The *Nine-O-Nine* B-17 bomber flew 140 bombing missions over the ETO without a casualty, killed or wounded. The *5 Grand*, another B-17, was the 5,000th Seattle-built Boeing and bore the signatures of the workers there. While at Dow, the young airmen relaxed and reveled in being home before

Airmen inspect damage to the nose turret of B-17 *Nine-O-Nine* caused by a German eighty-eight-millimeter shell. *Bangor Public Library.*

their redeployment to the PTO (Pacific Theater of Operations). Despite this reprieve in wartime activity, the Pacific war continued unabated. The bloody attack on Okinawa, one of Japan's home islands, begun in April horrified Americans. Desperate Japanese pilots flew their aircraft against American ships in suicidal attacks while their armies dug deep into the land in defensive positions.[123]

In Bangor that summer, war was still very much a reality. Rationing of gasoline and food commodities, particularly meat and sugar, continued. Bangoreans planted victory gardens again as they had all through the war. The city set aside four acres of land off Webster Avenue for residents without enough land around their houses to use for a garden. James Stanley and his wife used land set aside off Mt. Hope Avenue across from the State Hospital. "You simply had to go to city hall and get a plot of land assigned," recalled Stanley.[124] At harvest, residents could bring their produce for canning to a canning center set up at Bangor High School under the auspices of the Bangor Civil Defense office. In return for this service, residents donated one processed canning jar out of five to the Bangor school lunch program.

Above: The *5 Grand* and crew. This B-17 served with the 96th Bombardment Group. *Bangor Historical Society.*

Right: Young airmen glad to be home and enjoying fresh milk at Dow Field Post Exchange. *Bangor Public Library.*

The soldiers at Dow Field also had a victory garden of ten acres and in the summer of 1944 donated forty bushels of corn to the canning center for processing. The chamber of commerce encouraged citizens to band together in victory garden clubs and tend a large victory garden. In the summer of 1944, the chamber awarded a unique plaque to the Strickland Farm Little City Garden Club, a group of fifty-one neighborhood gardeners.

For the military personnel, it was war as usual at Dow Field. Returning aircraft continued to filter through the air base. Lieutenant Colonel Schurter left in early June to assume command of the ATC base in Goose Bay, Labrador. Lieutenant Colonel Edward F. Tindall replaced him as base commander. One of his first duties was to oversee the reassignment of the 451st Bombardment Group to Dow Field. The 451st, composed of more than 2,000 airmen, distinguished itself as part of the 15th Air Force with three Presidential Citations for their part in bombing raids on Regensburg, Germany; Ploesti, Romania; and Markesdorf, Austria. Colonel Tindall also hosted an open house in late June. More than 30,000 local residents attended the event, toured the facilities, viewed demonstrations and watched an airborne show. But later that summer, Colonel Tindall hosted a different sort of guest: 350 German prisoners of war. The First Service Command assigned the POWs from the large camp in Houlton to Dow Field to help in the local harvesting of farm crops. An advance party of POWs set up a stockade with four guard towers on the north side of the base along Union Street. Prisoners occupied barracks used previously by

The price of war: a 451st Bomb Group B-24 bomber engulfed by flame after attack by German fighters. The bomber soon exploded with all lost. *Lee Sirabella.*

Bangoreans enjoy a base open house, June 1945. *Richard R. Shaw.*

engineers before their deployment. Curiously, military officials did not transport the Germans through Union Station but brought them to the base over the Dow Field railroad spur on the Hammond Street side and unloaded them at the quartermaster warehouses there.

Stark and simple: German prisoners' barracks at Dow Field. *Lee Sirabella.*

German prisoners at Dow Field. Captured in North Africa, these men returned to a country devastated by war, thanks to Hitler. *Bangor Public Library.*

July 4 was very quiet in Bangor that year. Bangoreans wondered what was next in the war with Japan. President Truman, meeting a few days later with Allied leaders in Potsdam, Germany, learned of the successful test of a new American bomb. Only weeks later, the army air forces dropped this new "atomic" bomb on the Japanese cities of Hiroshima and Nagasaki. Emperor Hirohito, in a god-like move to save his people from total destruction, agreed to surrender terms. The Second World War was over.

CONCLUSION

"Make it bigger!" yelled soldiers as they left the Penobscot Hotel across from the Exchange Street office of the *Bangor Daily News*. There, an employee had posted a sign in the window that read, "WAR ENDS." It was 7:15 p.m., Tuesday evening, August 14; a few minutes before in Washington, President Truman had announced that the Japanese had agreed to surrender terms. This news spread like wildfire through the river city. Church bells pealed, and fire alarms screamed. Bangoreans flooded their streets. Cars, little used during the war, jammed the roadways. An ordered pandemonium followed as citizens came together in joyful celebration.

The chamber of commerce's Norbert Dowd, in keeping with the president's designation of August 15 and 16 as legal holidays, announced that all Bangor businesses were closed. Bangoreans simply celebrated in the downtown streets, shooting off fireworks and making noise with whatever they could find. City police and Dow Field MPs looked on but were not needed. And people went to their houses of worship for special services of thanksgiving.

At Dow Field, Colonel Tindall presided over a special Wednesday morning ceremony in front of base headquarters. He shared an enlisted man's quip that "we won the war in spite of the officers" with the five hundred gathered there. But he later spoke for all, citizens and soldiers, when he said, "We may all feel justly proud of our individual contributions."

Colonel Tindall reflected on the sentiment that won the war: all Americans came together and worked for a common goal—victory. In its

Impromptu victory parade in downtown Bangor, August 14, 1945. *Richard R. Shaw.*

unique corner of the country, Bangor especially epitomized this national goal. Here, citizens and soldiers banded together, first for defense, then for victory. Dow Field emerged as a tangible instrument in the country's war plans. Now, with long-term peace in the offing, the future of Bangor's air base lay in doubt. Unfolding events proved, though, that world peace was an elusive goal for mankind and that Dow Field would have a renewed purpose. That history is another story of people and place.

NOTES

Introduction

1. Report of Municipal Services, Bangor, Maine, 1947.
2. *Bangor Daily News*, May 31–June 1, 1947.

Chapter 1

3. Unless noted otherwise, information for this chapter is taken from the *Bangor Daily News* or the *Bangor Daily Commercial*, May 27, 1919, to January 27, 1940.
4. *Bangor Daily Commercial*, obituary, May 21, 1937.
5. Miller, *Billy Mitchell*, 89.
6. Dorr, *Mission to Tokyo*, 23.
7. Vickery, *Illustrated History*, 75.
8. *Bangor Daily News*, obituary, December 3, 1958, 1.
9. City of Bangor Directory, 1927.
10. City of Bangor, Municipal Activities Annual Reports, 1936 and 1937.

Chapter 2

11. Roosevelt, *Rendezvous With Destiny*, 273–74.
12. PBS, *The War: War Production*, www.pbs.org/thewar/at_home_war_production.htm.

13. Linton, *American Almanac*, 348.
14. Unless noted otherwise, information for this chapter is taken from the *Bangor Daily News* or the *Bangor Daily Commercial*, March 6, 1940, to May 30, 1941.
15. Dear, *Oxford Guide*, 919.
16. Thompson, "Brief History," 2.

CHAPTER 3

17. *Bangor Daily News*, February 15, 1941.
18. Ibid., November 12, 1940.
19. Dear, *Oxford Guide*, 925.
20. Gloria Dow Pelletier, letter to the author, August 27, 2008.
21. Ellen D. Cotton (James Dow's niece), letter to the author, March 13, 2008.
22. Pelletier, letter.
23. Unless otherwise noted, information for this chapter is taken from the story written by the author titled "Houlton's Speed King" in *Echoes Magazine: The Northern Maine Journal* no. 81 (July–September 2008).
24. Pelletier, letter.
25. Hebron Academy Yearbook, *The Green Parrot* (1932), 45.
26. *Bangor Daily News*, May 19, 1942.
27. Pelletier, letter.
28. Ibid.
29. James F. Dow, letter to his parents, March 19, 1940.
30. The official accident report compiled by the air corps was lost. This account is constructed from eyewitness reports that appeared in the Tuesday, June 18 issues of the *New York Times*, *New York Herald Tribune* and *Daily News*. The newspapers also included the eyewitness account of Lieutenant Ellis, who saw this incident unfold before him.
31. Pelletier, letter.

CHAPTER 4

32. Dear, *Oxford Guide*, 1023.
33. Unless otherwise noted, information for this chapter is taken from the *Bangor Daily News* or the *Bangor Daily Commercial*, February 4, 1941, to November 26, 1941.

34. *Bangor Daily News,* August 8, 1944.
35. Thompson, "Brief History," 14.
36. City of Bangor, Municipal Activities Annual Report, 1936.
37. *Bangor Daily News*, September 19, 1940.
38. The army listed General Dargue and seven other army personnel as missing on a transcontinental flight on December 18, 1941. The last radio contact with the aircraft occurred two miles south of Palmdale, California.
39. *Bangor Daily News*, August 8, 1944.
40. *Life Magazine*, July 7, 1941, 95.
41. Dear, *Oxford Guide*, 920.
42. Roosevelt, *Memorable Quotations*, 227.

CHAPTER 5

43. James S. Stanley, interview with the author, November 10, 2014.
44. Bangor Service Record, Bangor Public Library, 1946.
45. Unless otherwise noted, information for this chapter is taken from the *Bangor Daily News* or the *Bangor Daily Commercial*, December 8, 1941, to July 10, 1942.
46. Linton, *American Almanac*, 354.
47. Maurer, *Air Force Combat Units*, 99.
48. Air Force Historical Research Agency, *History of Dow Field.*
49. Stanley, interview.
50. *Bangor Daily News*, June 3, 1940. Rickenbacker would follow his own advice. During the war, he served as a valuable consultant for the army air forces and toured strategic military outposts. On one such trip in October 1942, the B-17 in which he was a passenger missed its island destination in the vast South Pacific and crashed into the ocean. He survived twenty-four days floating about in a five-man raft until rescued by a U.S. Navy search party. This amazing wartime story is included in his autobiography titled *Rickenbacker: An Autobiography*.
51. *Life Magazine*, July 7, 1941, 34–35.

CHAPTER 6

52. Unless otherwise noted, information for this chapter is taken from the *Bangor Daily News* or the *Bangor Daily Commercial*, May 31, 1941, to March 28, 1945.

53. *Bangor Daily News*, November 13, 1941.
54. Ibid., December 25, 2013.

CHAPTER 7

55. Air Force Historical Research Agency, *History of Dow Field.*
56. Ibid.
57. Thompson, "Brief History," 3–4.
58. Maurer, *Air Force Combat Units*, 166.
59. Air Force Historical Research Agency, *History of Dow Field.*
60. Unless otherwise noted, information for this chapter is taken from the *Bangor Daily News* or the *Bangor Daily Commercial*, May 16, 1941, to November 29, 1942.
61. Stanley, interview.
62. Morgan, *Man Who Flew*, 96.
63. Ibid., 98–99.
64. Miller, *Masters of the Air*, 48, 54, 127, 145–47.
65. Thompson, "Brief History," 4–5.
66. Air Force Historical Research Agency, *History of Dow Field.*
67. Stanley, interview.
68. *Bangor Daily News*, October 5, 1942.
69. Linton, *American Almanac*, 354–55.
70. Thompson, "Brief History," 5.

CHAPTER 8

71. *New York Times*, "House Votes War; Miss Rankin 'Nay,'" December 6, 1941, 6.
72. Unless otherwise noted, information for this chapter is taken from the *Bangor Daily News* or the *Bangor Daily Commercial*, October 9, 1942, to May 4, 1945.
73. *Dow Field Observer*, December 28, 1942.
74. Air Force Historical Research Agency, *History of Dow Field.*
75. *Dow Field Observer*, October 18, 1943.
76. Ibid., January 3, 1944.
77. Ibid., December 28, 1942.

CHAPTER 9

78. Audio tape of *The Jack Benny Show*, January 3, 1943, Bangor, Maine.
79. Unless otherwise noted, information for this chapter is taken from the *Bangor Daily News* or the *Bangor Daily Commercial* from August 4, 1941, to June 7, 1944.
80. Thompson, "Brief History," 6.
81. Air Force Historical Research Agency, *History of Dow Field.*
82. Dear, *Oxford Guide*, 1028.
83. Murray and Millett, *War to Be Won*, 317.
84. Dugan and Stewart, *Ploesti*, 38–39.
85. Craven and Cate, *Army Air Forces*, 477–78.
86. Ibid., 481.
87. Dugan and Stewart, *Ploesti*, 106.
88. Craven and Cate, *Army Air Forces*, 482–83.
89. Dear, *Oxford Guide*, 1029–30.
90. Air Force Historical Research Agency, *History of Dow Field.*
91. Ibid.
92. Dear, *Oxford Guide*, 1030–31.
93. *Dow Field Observer*, March 21, 1945.
94. Air Force Historical Research Agency, *History of Dow Field.*
95. Thompson, "Brief History," 7.

CHAPTER 10

96. Unless otherwise noted, information for this chapter is taken from the *Bangor Daily News* or *Bangor Daily Commercial*, February 27, 1940, to December 20, 1944. In July 1944, the *Bangor Daily News* assigned managing editor John M. O'Connell to cover war news in Europe. His column, titled "Victory Bound With Our Maine Boys," became a daily feature with the newspaper for the remainder of the war and provides a unique insight into the ETO.
97. Murray and Millett, *War to Be Won*, 250.
98. David H. Bergquist, "Wings Over Dow: A Story of Wartime Love and Heartache," *Echoes Magazine: The Northern Maine Journal* no. 89 (July–September 2010).
99. William B. Bunga to Edgar N. Keith, November 27, 1945, author's collection.
100. The story of Bangor's Austin Rodney Keith is told in the book *Prelude to Courage: An Air Warrior's Journey of Faith* by the author.

CHAPTER 11

101. Freeman, *B-17 Flying Fortress*, 239.
102. War Department, U.S. Army Air Forces, Report of Aircraft Accident, #43-38023.
103. *Portland Press Herald*, "Cloudburst Hits Waterville Area," July 12, 1944.
104. Art Pachen (Cecil Murphy's cousin), telephone conversation with the author, September 19, 2008.
105. Ibid.
106. *Bangor Daily News*, "Like a Giant Lawnmower Went Through Here," July 11, 2014.
107. *Bangor Daily News*, "Major Robert L. Simons in Charge of Operation at Dow Field," September 9, 1944.
108. *Bangor Daily News*, August 18, 1943.
109. Thompson, "Brief History," 8.
110. Air Force Historical Research Agency, *History of Dow Field.*
111. Ibid.
112. Unless otherwise noted, information for this chapter and conclusion is taken from the *Bangor Daily News* or *Bangor Daily Commercial*, June 4, 1943, to August 31, 1945.
113. Air Force Historical Research Agency, *History of Dow Field.*
114. Linton, *American Almanac*, 360.
115. Lee Sirabella, interview, October 28, 2014.
116. Dear, *Oxford Guide*, 1031–32.
117. Thompson, "Brief History," 9.
118. Lee Sirabella, e-mail notes, January 26, 2015.
119. Linton, *American Almanac*, 360.
120. Ibid., 361.
121. Horace E. Estey, 13th Annual Report of the City of Bangor of Bangor, 48.
122. Linton, *American Almanac*, 361.
123. Ibid.
124. Stanley, interview.

BIBLIOGRAPHY

Air Force Historical Research Agency. *History of Dow Field.* AFHRA Microfilm Reel, B2163.

Bergquist, David H. *Prelude to Courage: An Air Warrior's Journey of Faith.* Westminster, MD: Heritage Books, 2011.

Blanding, Edward M. *The City of Bangor.* Bangor, ME: Press of the Industrial Journal, 1899.

Carman, Harry J. *History of the American People.* Vol. 2. New York: Alfred A. Knopf, 1961.

Craven, Wesley F., and James L. Cate. *The Army Air Forces in World War II.* Vol. 2. Chicago: University of Chicago Press, 1956.

Dear, I.C.B. *The Oxford Guide to World War II.* Oxford, UK: Oxford University Press, 1995.

Dorr, Robert F. *Mission to Tokyo.* Minneapolis, MN: Zenith Press, 2012.

Dugan, James, and Carol Stewart. *Ploesti: The Great Ground-Air Battle of 1 August 1943.* Washington, D.C.: Brassey's, Inc., 2002.

Eden, Paul. *The Encyclopedia of Aircraft of WWII.* London: Amber Books, 2004.

Freeman, Roger A. *The B-17 Flying Fortress Story.* London: Arms and Armour Press, 1998.

Garbinski, John C. *The United States Air Force in Maine.* Bangor: Maine Aviation Historical Society, 1998.

Linton, Calvin D. *The American Almanac.* Nashville, TN: Thomas Nelson Inc., 1977.

Maurer, Maurer. *Air Force Combat Units of World War II*. Edison, NJ: Chartwell Books, 1994.

Miller, Donald L. *Masters of the Air*. New York: Simon and Schuster, 2006.

———. *The Story of World War II*. New York: Simon and Schuster, 2001.

Miller, Roger C. *Billy Mitchell: Evangelist of AirPower*. Stockton, NJ: OTTN Publishing, 2008.

Morgan, Robert. *The Man Who Flew the Memphis Belle*. New York: Dutton, 2001.

Murray, Williamson, and Allan R. Millett. *A War to Be Won*. Cambridge, MA: Belknap Press, 2000.

Rickenbacker, Edward V. *Rickenbacker*. Englewood Cliffs, NJ: Prentice-Hall, 1967.

Roosevelt, Elliott. *As He Saw It*. New York: Duell, Sloan and Pearce, 1946.

Roosevelt, Franklin Delano. *Memorable Quotations of Franklin D. Roosevelt*. New York: Thomas Y. Crowell Co., 1965.

———. *Rendezvous With Destiny: Addresses and Opinions of Franklin Delano Roosevelt*. Edited by J.B.S. Hardman. New York: Dryden Press, 1944.

Thompson, A.G. "A Brief History of Dow Field." Unpublished manuscript, Bangor Room, Bangor Public Library, 1946.

Vickery, James B. *An Illustrated History of the City of Bangor*. Bangor, ME: Bangor Bi-Centennial Committee, 1976.

Zelz, Abigail E., and Marilyn Zoidis. *Woodsmen and Whigs: Historical Images of Bangor, Maine*. Virginia Beach, VA: Donning Company, 1991.

INDEX

C

D

E

F

G

H

J

K

L

R

S

T

U

V

W

Y

ABOUT THE AUTHOR

David H. Bergquist lives and writes in Hermon, Maine, following a nearly fifty-year career in education. With bachelor's and master's degrees from the University of Maine and a doctorate from the University of Nebraska, he served for thirty years as a college administrator for Becker College, retiring in 2003 as dean. He is an avid historian and frequently writes and lectures about World War II history. His first book, *Prelude to Courage: An Air Warrior's Journey of Faith*, was published in 2011 by Heritage Books, Inc.